Drawing Basics

Simple drawing projects for beginners

Marco T. Brand

Table of Contents

Disclaimer

While all attempts have been made to verify the information provided in this book, the author does assume any responsibility for errors, omissions, or contrary interpretations of the subject matter contained within. The information provided in this book is for educational and entertainment purposes only. The reader is responsible for his or her own actions and the author does not accept any responsibilities for any liabilities or damages, real or perceived, resulting from the use of this information.

The trademarks that are used are without any consent, and the publication of the trademark is without permission or backing by the trademark owner. All trademarks and brands within this book are for clarifying purposes only and are the owned by the owners themselves, not affiliated with this document.

You don't know where to start...

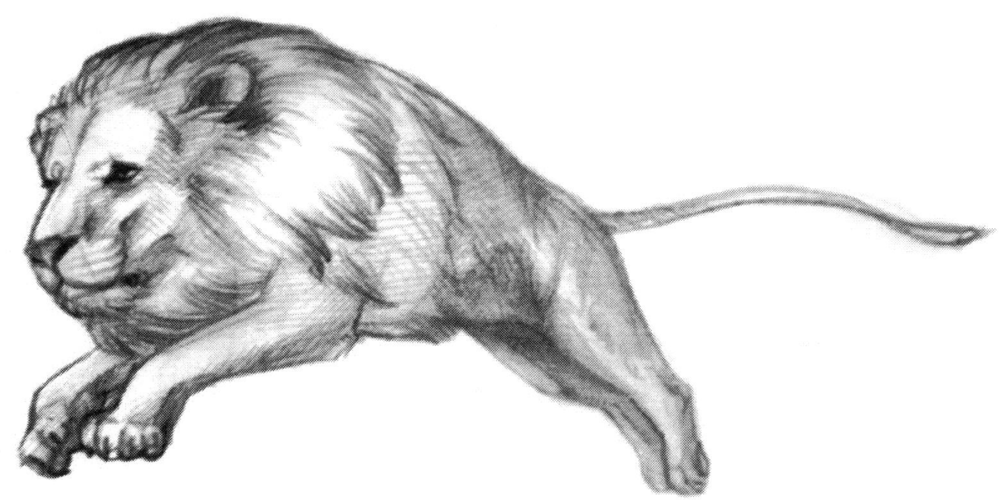

You've tried to figure out how to draw and have gotten frustrated when your attempts have fallen short from what you think your project should look like. You've gone online to find tutorials and download books on how to do it, but the videos are constantly making you pause them and back them up, or the books you try to follow leave out steps, making you guess at how they did it.

I understand, and that is why I formatted and wrote this book. This book will answer all your questions about shading, perspective, and basic drawing by using step-by-step instructions down to the smallest detail. I start with what you will need to get started, move on to basic techniques, and then we dive into the projects. So if you're ready to learn how to draw, what are you waiting for?

Let's get started!

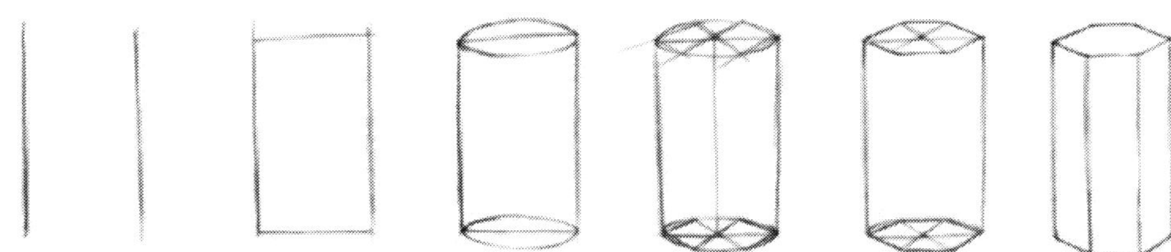

This book has been structured to walk you through every step of the drawing process. I have written it to include answers to commonly asked questions for people just getting started. This book will:

- Walk you through what you will need to get started with your new hobby.

- Go step by step on how to shade, draw perspective drawings, and basic shapes.

- Walk you through basic anatomy drawings

- Walk you through several exercises for many different projects.

- Give you extra projects you can work on yourself.

So, if you are ready to roll up your sleeves and learn about a new and rewarding hobby, swipe the page and let's get started!

Chapter 1 - Things to keep in mind during drawing

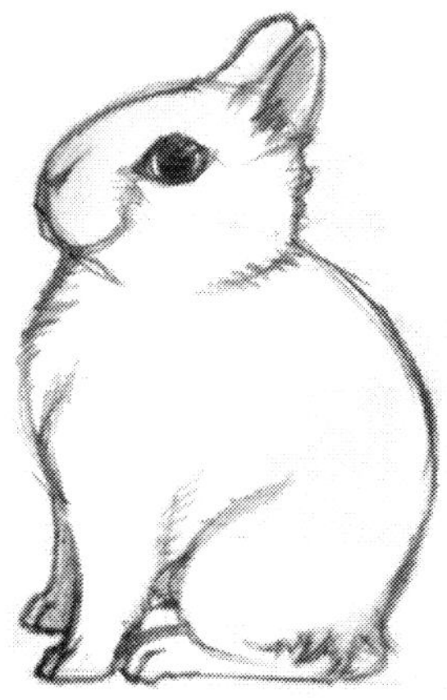

We all attack something new with curiosity and exuberance, but in our excitement, we tend to get frustrated, sometimes to the point of quitting before we really get going. Here are a few pieces of advice:

You're just getting started

I know this seems obvious, but I feel it needs to be said. We often go into new hobbies with a notion of how it is supposed to go, but when we start, and it doesn't go our way, we get frustrated. Just remember, everything goes slowly at first, and the speed will come later.

It won't be perfect at first

It will take more than one try to get something right. So, don't get mad at yourself if it does not turn out right at first. If you have to repeat the same exercise more than once, go for it. Work at your own pace. It's not a race.

Don't refer to any other person's work

We want to look at other people's artwork and compare our work to theirs. Try not to do that. Everyone has their own style and yours may not be the same as the person's who work you are looking at. In order to get a good look at how far you are progressing, look at your previous work and compare it to what you're doing at present. Never lose track of the fact the people you admire for their work has been practicing their art for months and even years.

Never stop practicing

When you are through with this book and its exercises, go back and do some of them again as a refresher, practice, or just for fun. Also, take pictures of things you are interested in drawing to practice drawing them later. Challenge yourself with things to draw that are out of your comfort zone.

Chapter 2 - Your shopping list for draw

As a mechanic needs socket wrenches and other things to do their trade, you will need a basic set of tools to be ready for your new hobby.

The basics drawing

Pencils

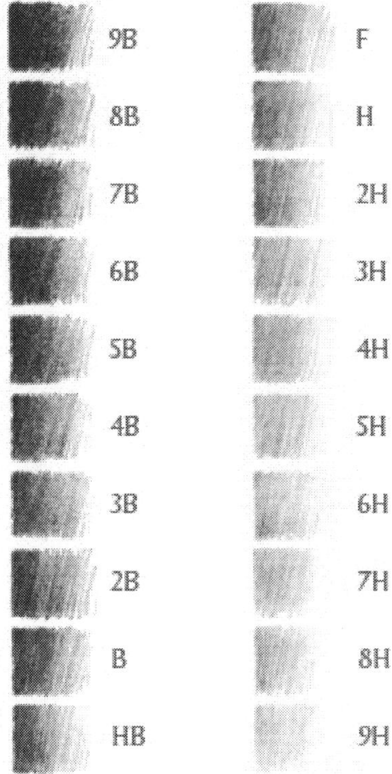

A mechanical pencil with HB lead or a No. 2 pencil will do to start. When you want to branch out for more difficult projects, there are pencil sets and other leads you can use for your mechanical pencils for outlining and shading. The tables you see above are all the different types of lead that are available for drawing.

Erasers

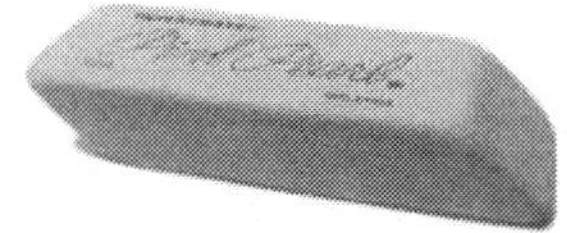

From gray erasers that you can use to smudge and white erasers for ink, there are different types, and they each have their own uses. For now, using a simple pink eraser will do for now.

Sketch Pad

Go for the affordable pad you can get at dollar stores and such to start out. You can even use notebook paper. Later on, you can buy the higher grade sketch paper and pads.

Chair

A comfortable chair is important as you will be sitting for long periods of time. Make sure the chair is rated for being comfortable for hours on end.

Table/Desk

Your table or desk needs to be at a level where you are comfortable working at. It also needs to be at a level to prevent your arms and hands from falling asleep.

Lighting

Good lighting is very important. It needs to be soft on the page to prevent glare in the eyes. You don't need to feel like you are straining your eyes.

Kicking it up a level

If you are ready to go to the next level, there are a few things to add to your list.

Coloring tools

From chalks to colored markers, there are many options to choose from to color your projects when you are ready to add a little color.

T-Square

Many artists use this on a tilted table to hold there tools and helps with straight lines.

Triangles

You can use these to help with the more popular angles.

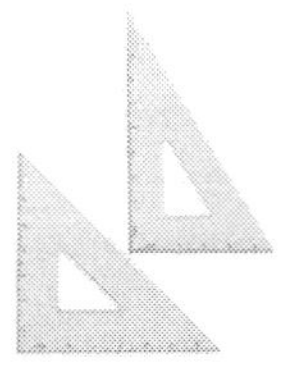

Ruler

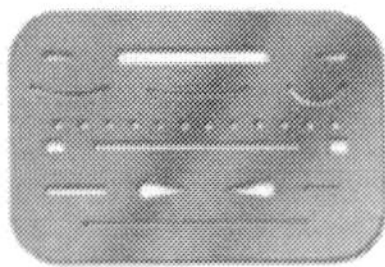

You can use this to mark measurements and help with lines in your projects.

Eraser guard

I use this to help me get rid of those tricky lines that are too close to lines I want to keep.

Horse Hair Brush

You can use this to clean off your paper without smudging your line work.

Smudge Sticks/Blending Stumps

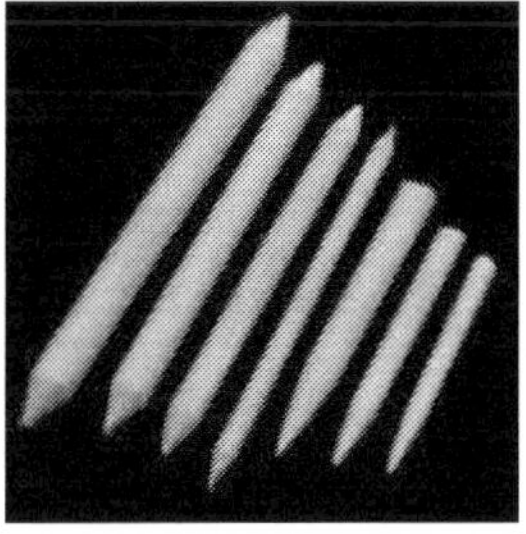

These are great for smoothing out shadows and blending shading.

Chapter 3 – Shading details

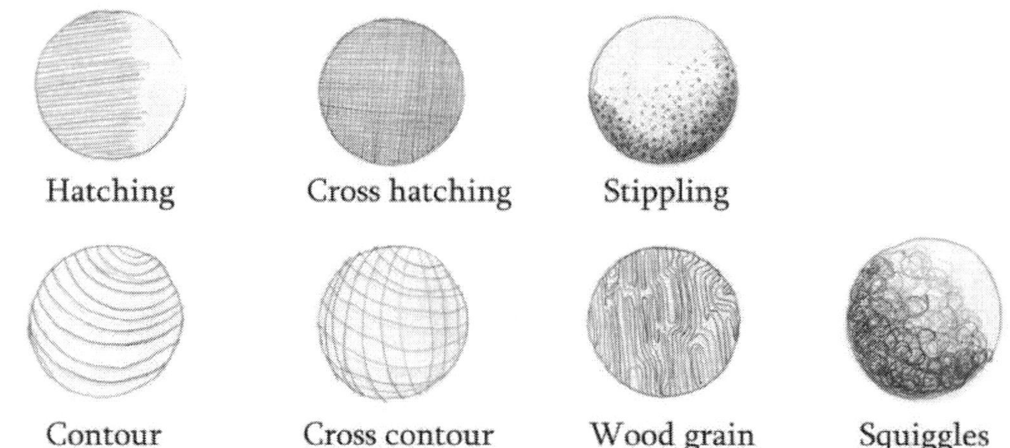

When you start learning how to draw, shading will play a part in putting details into your work. Here are a few techniques that are commonly used.

Hatching

These are quick, straight lines to show the direction of the shading in a picture.

Cross Hatching

These are lines that cross over one another to deepen the shading on an object or person.

Stippling

These are a rapid application of dots to show shading on an object or person.

Contour

Though they are shown as rounded lines, contouring can be used in this manner to show shapes in shading.

Cross Contour

This is an alternate form of cross hatching but using contour shading.

Wood grain

This is a series of curves, loops, and wavy lines that resemble wood grain and is used for shading in some projects.

Squiggles

These are a grouping of tightly squiggled lines for shading.

Casting your shadows

The above picture shows a typical way to shade an object, keeping in mind where the light source is originating from. As you can see, it is the lightest where the source comes in direct contact and the further from the light source it gets, the darker the shading becomes.

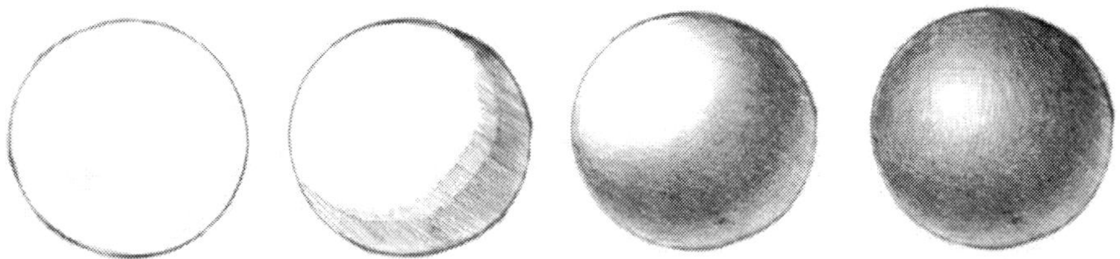

As you look at the picture on the left, pay particular attention to how the shadow falls from where the light source is. Try recreating the picture above.

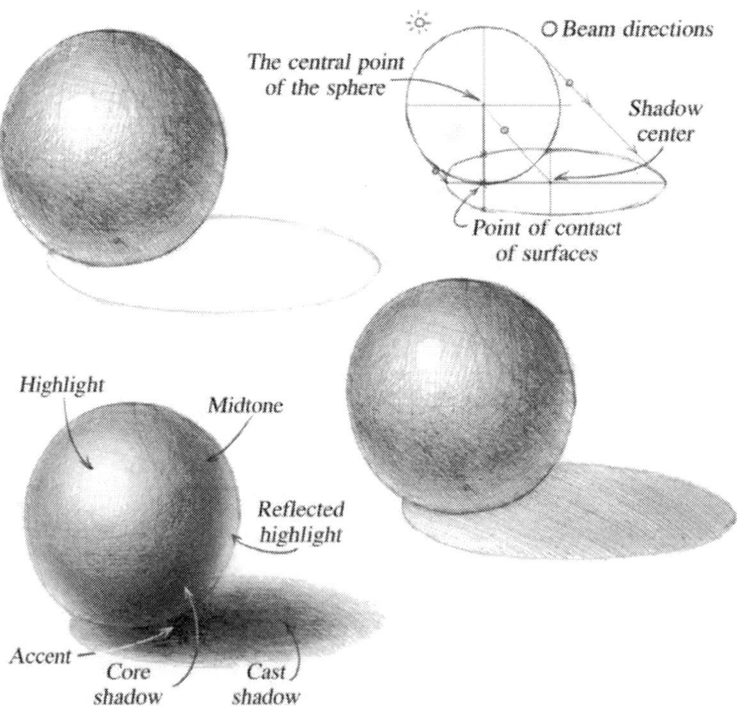

Chapter 4 – Figure drawing

Cylinder

Next exercise starts with making a cylinder. Like above, start from the left.

Draw your guides and use contour to shade.

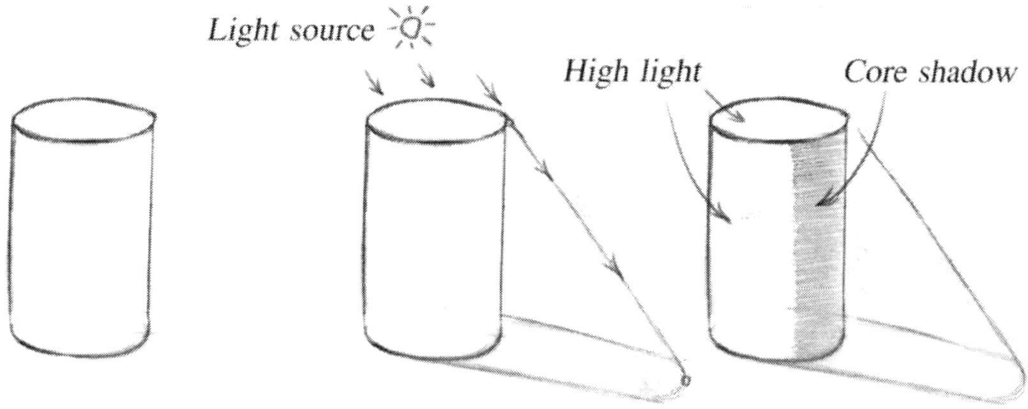

Pay attention to how the shading is placed on the cylinder. Smudge the shadow to get the book above.

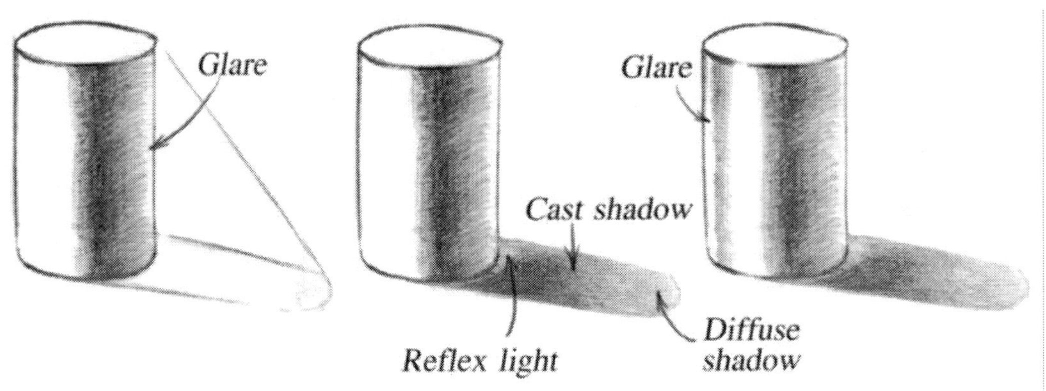
Glare
Glare
Cast shadow
Reflex light
Diffuse shadow

Cube

We are going to start with a simple cube.

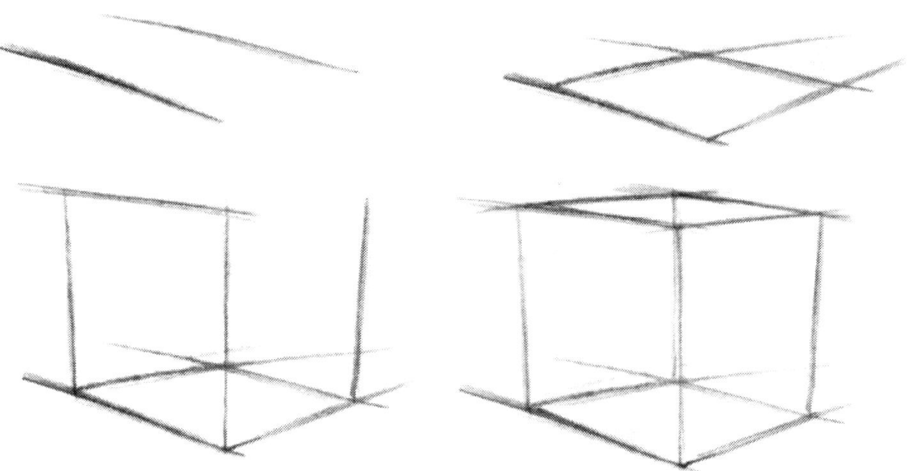

Here, we are refining the cube and laying the guide for the shadow.

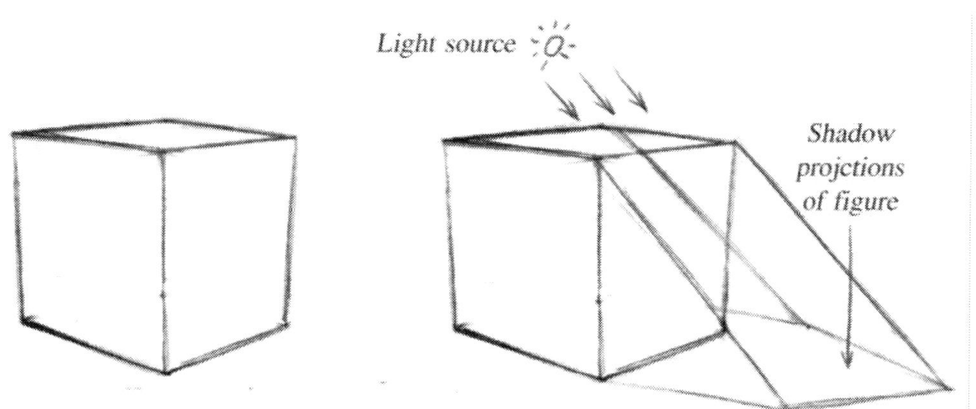

Starting on the left, use cross hatching to shade and blend the shading.

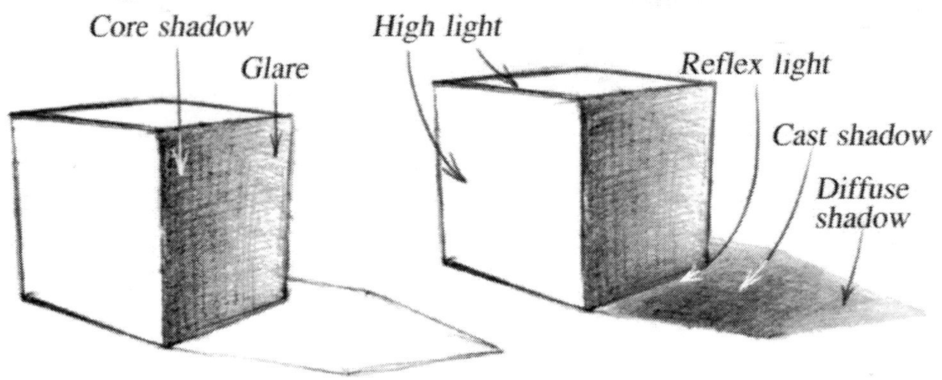
Core shadow
Glare
High light
Reflex light
Cast shadow
Diffuse
shadow

Hexagon

From the left to the right, draw the image above. Now, we are going to shade it.

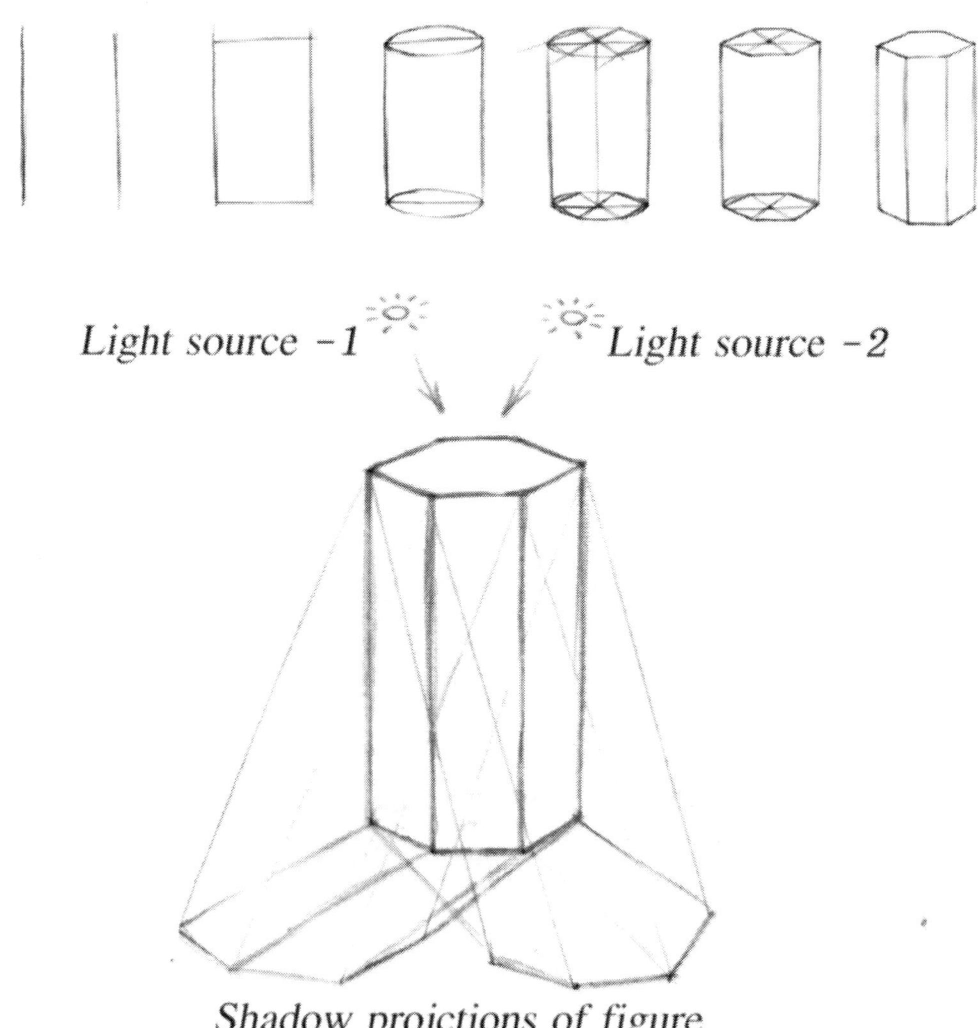

As you draw the lines down from the figure, take note of the light source. Keep the lines you use as a guide for the shadow edges light.

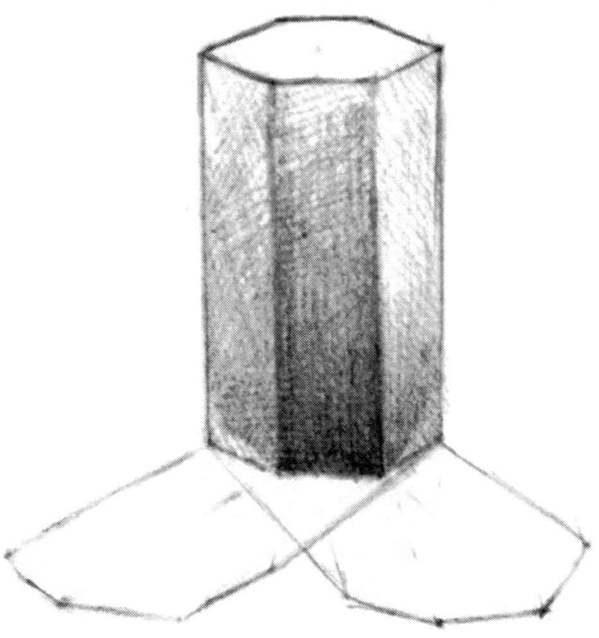

The easiest way to shade this would be to start at the bottom, and make you way toward the top. Then go over the darker parts of the figure to make them shaded as above.

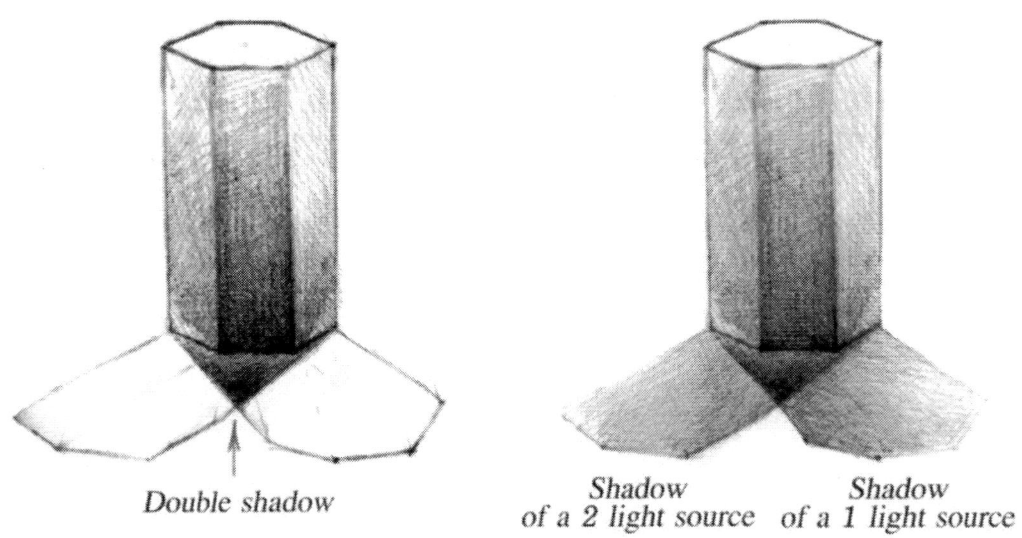

Use cross hatching to shade the figure starting on the left.

Cone

Make your shape above.

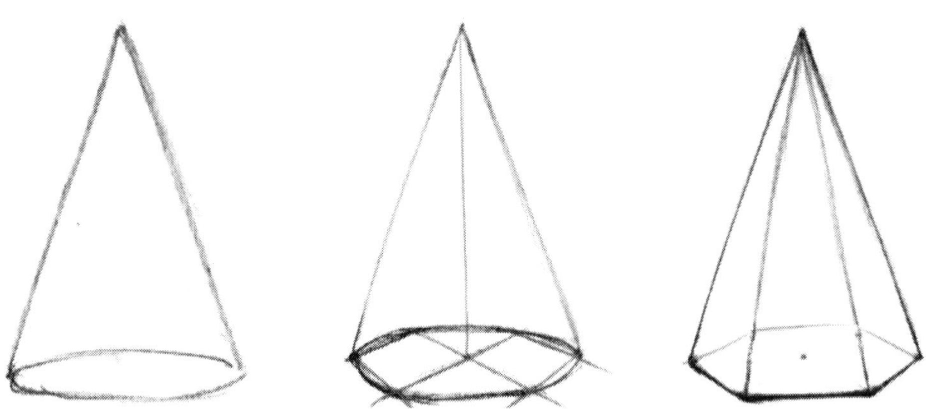

Notice you are shading two sides, and that we are shading before we lay the guides.

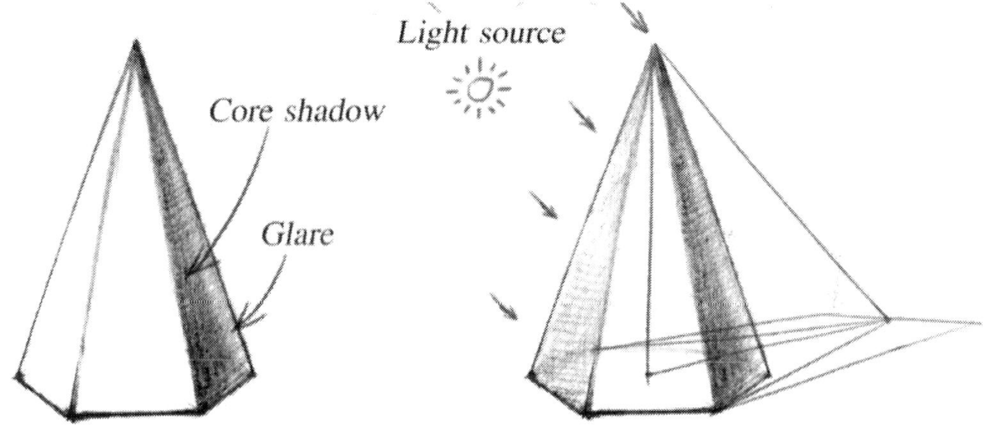

Play particular attention to how light the shading is on one side and much darker it is on the right side.

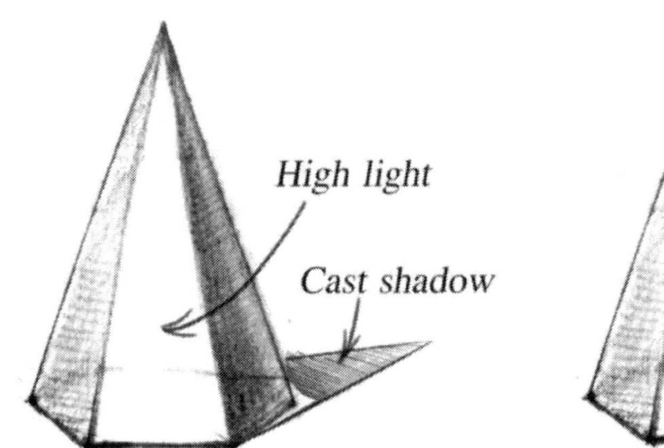
High light
Cast shadow

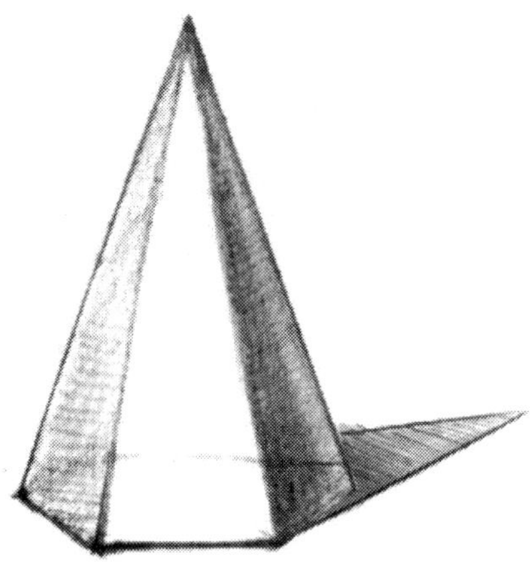

Chapter 5 – Perspective drawing

Perspective drawings add more depth and a 3D look for the drawing you want to do. This is also the technique draftsmen use to draw houses, cars, car parts, and other things to show more details.

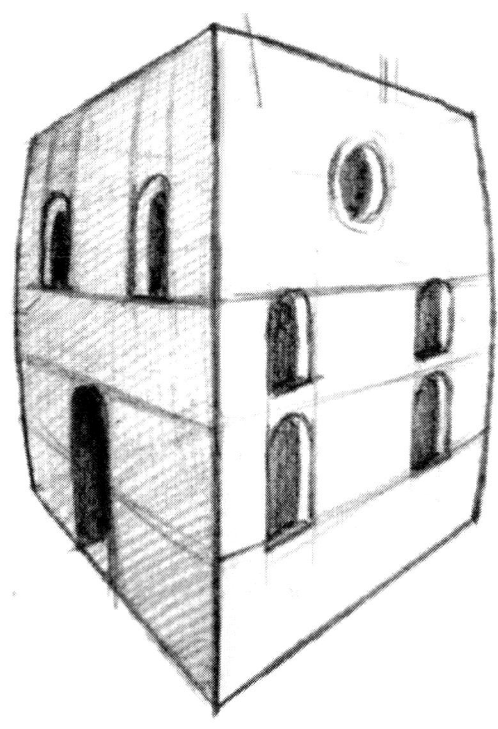

1. First you draw a straight line with the dot. This is the vanishing point for the picture.

2. These are the lines coming from the vanishing point.

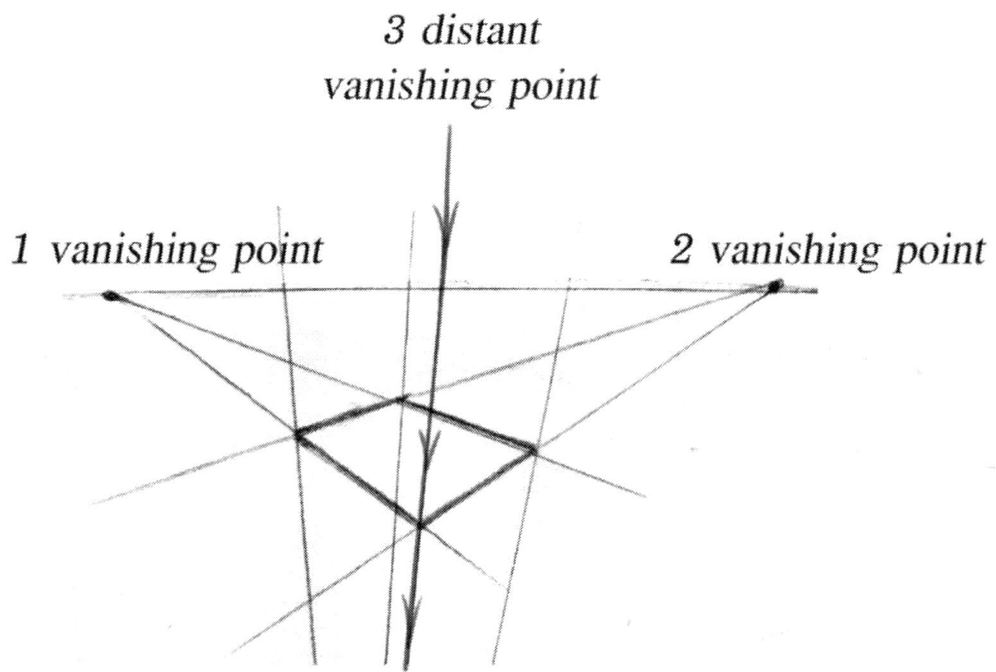

Take note of the second point on the left. The third vanishing point is not seen. Notice how the lines cross to make the bottom of the cube.

3. Add the lines for the corners.

4. Draw the top.

5. Erase the lines.

1. For this next exercise, once you've started your cube, add the fourth vanishing point.

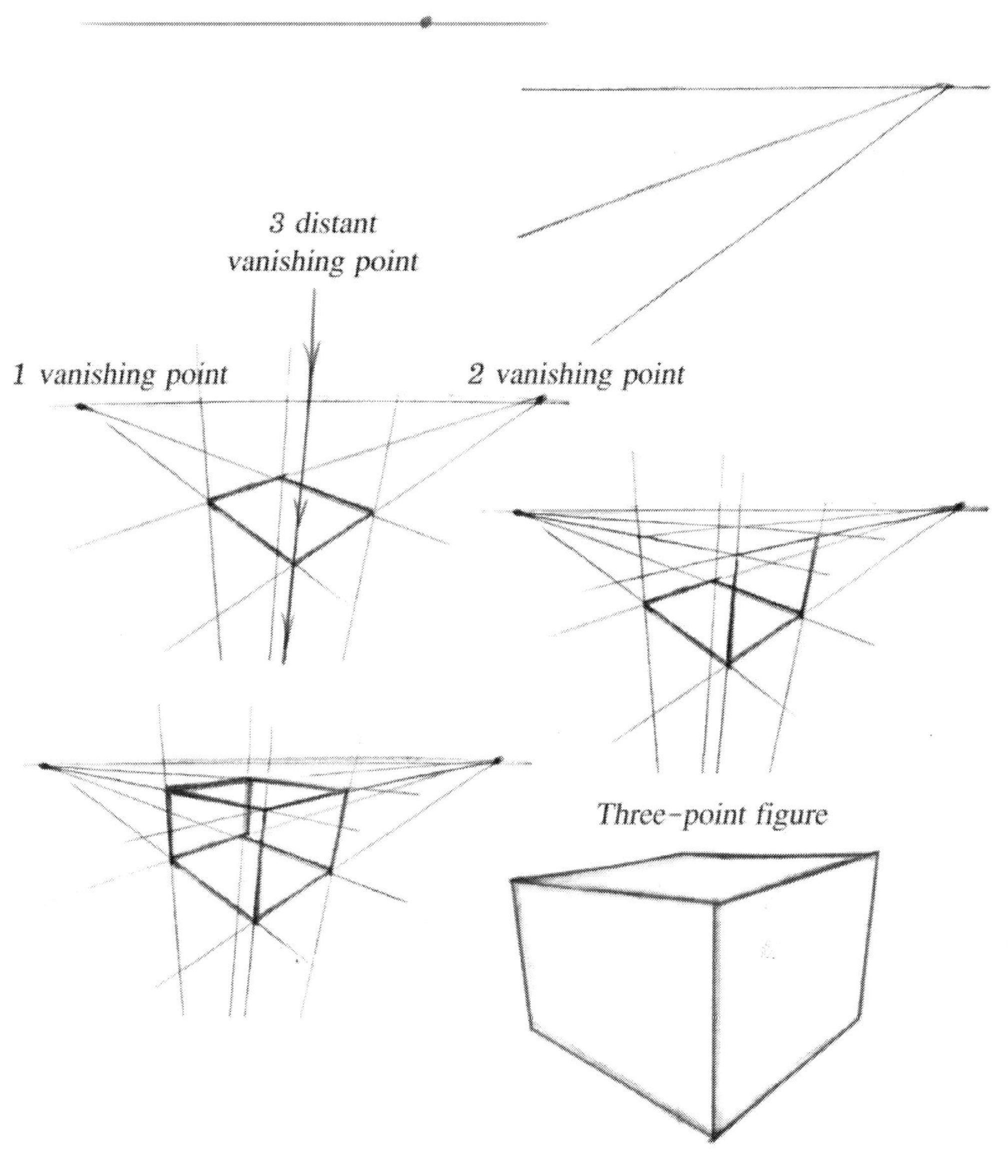

2. Make the lines as you see them in the picture.

3. Add the top of the structure.

Draw the rounded lines.

Add in your windows and door. Then clean it up for the finished product.

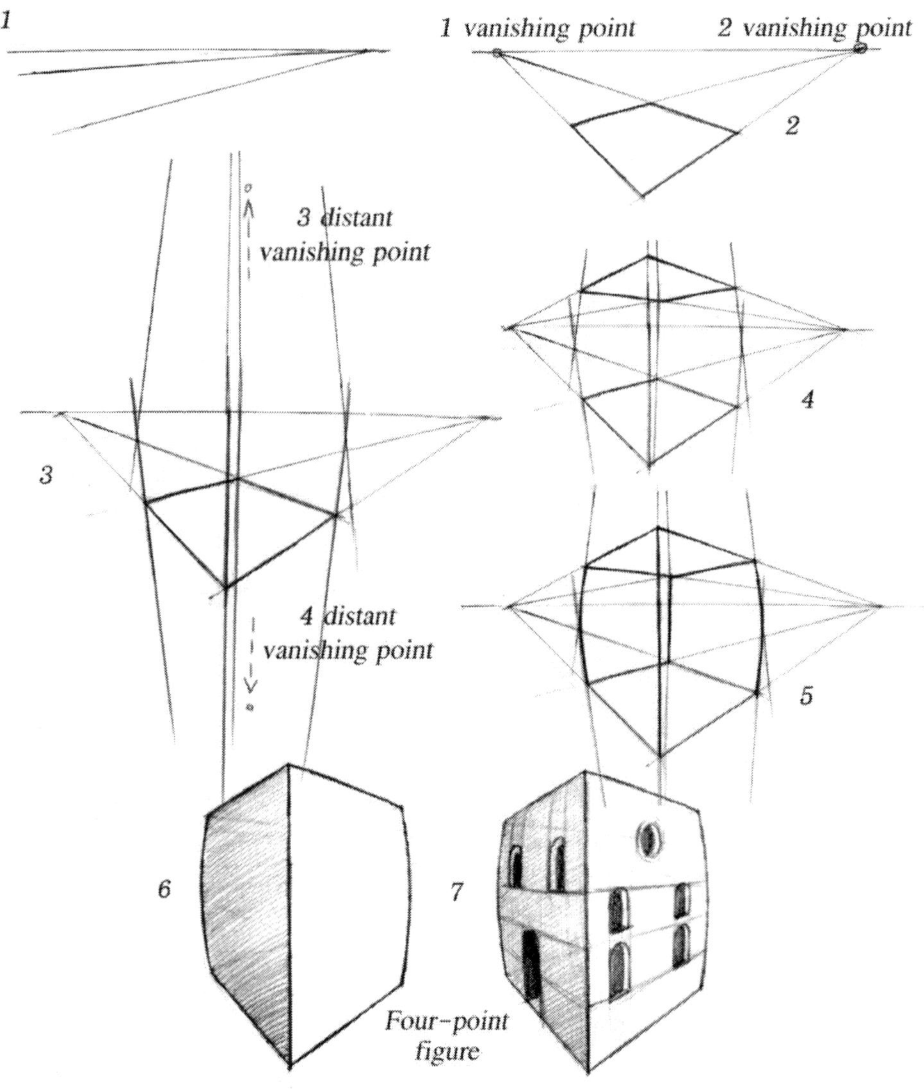

Starting is at the top left, make your vanishing points and then the 3D rectangle.

Extra practice

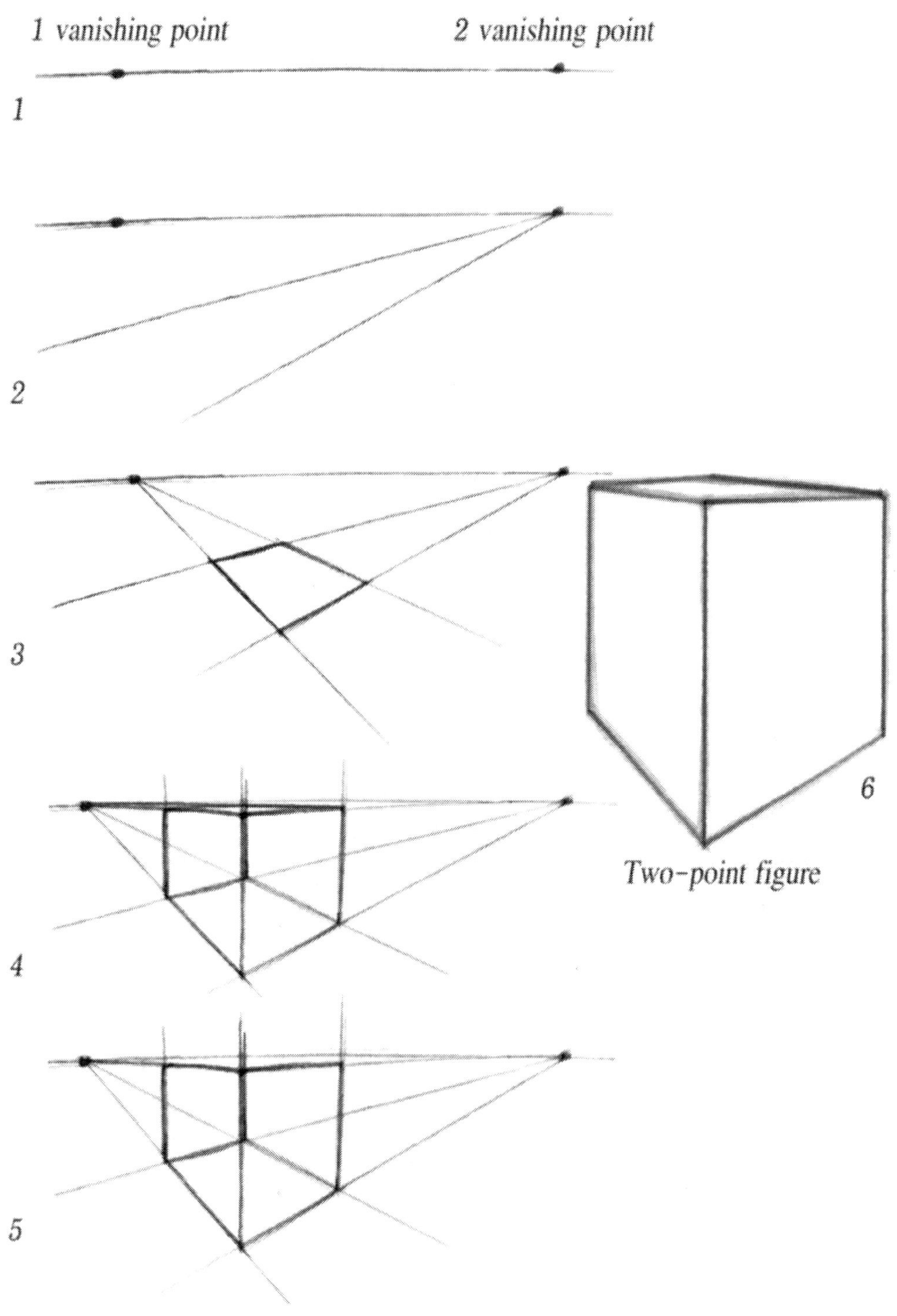

Two-point figure

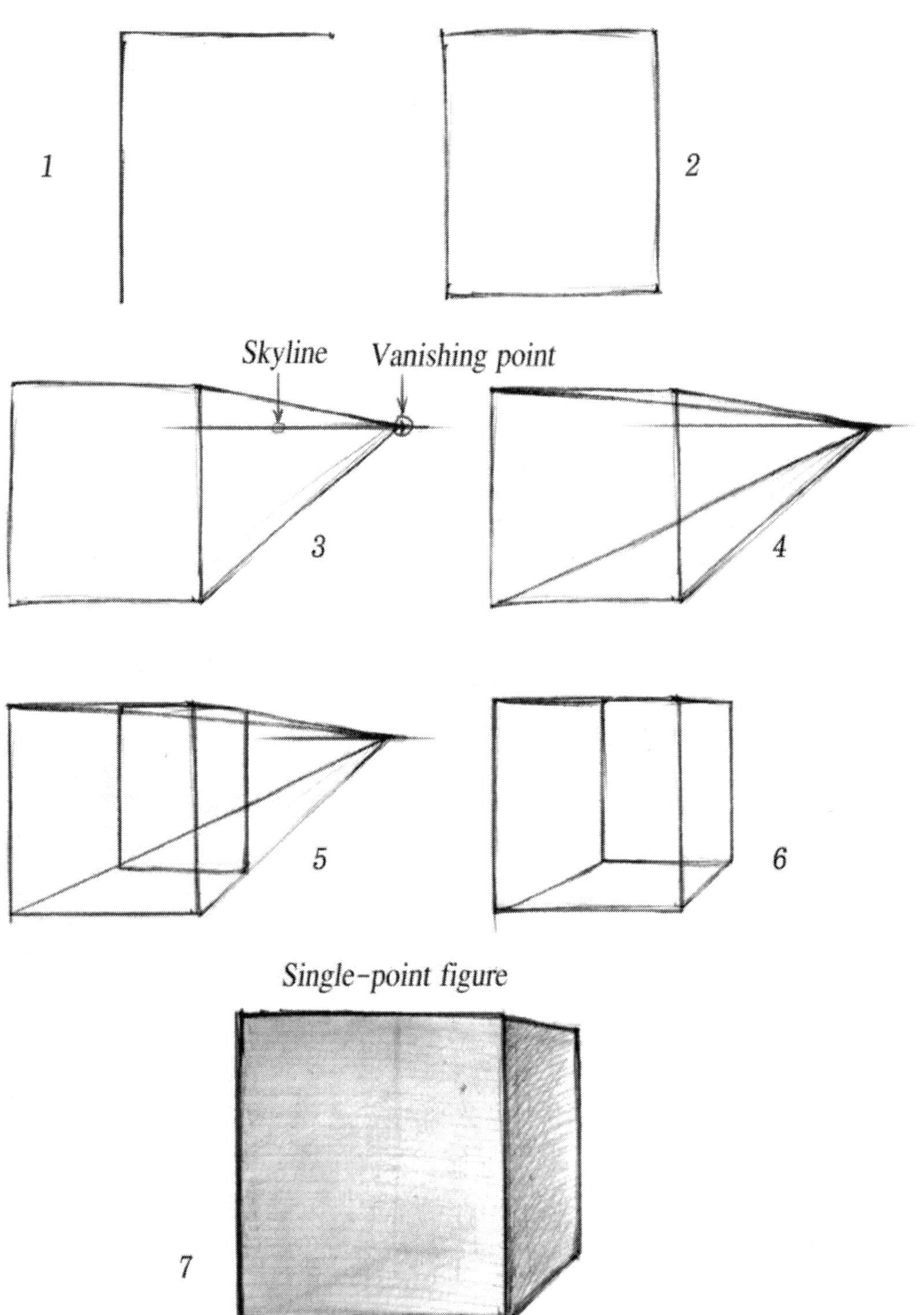
1
2
Skyline
Vanishing point
3
4
5
6
Single-point figure
7

Chapter 6 – Drawing cars

There is a certain way to draw cars so it doesn't seem like a chore or you're scratching your head wondering where to start.

Picture 1

1. Draw the rectangle you see here.

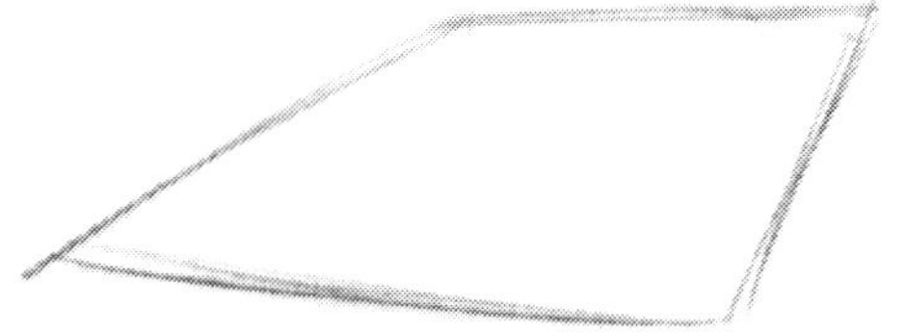

1. Draw the lines going up.

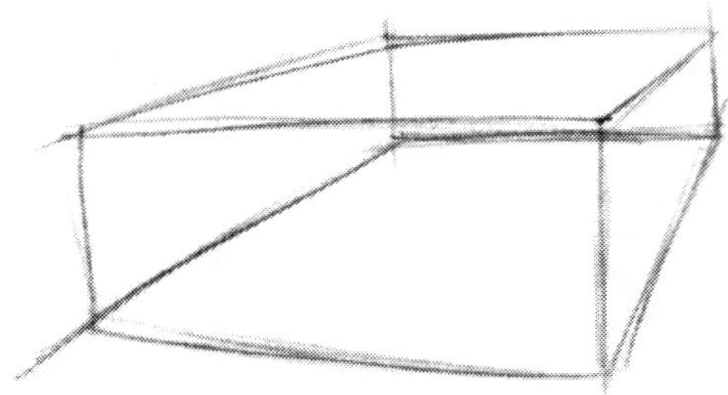

3. Add in the rectangle above the first.

4. Draw the rounded windshield.

5. Add the roof.

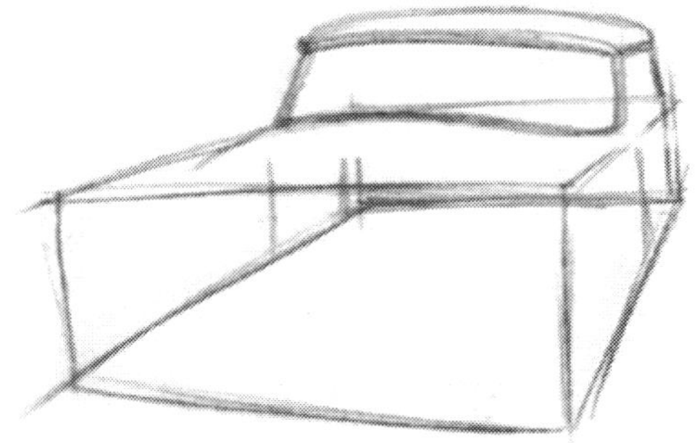

6. Add the line in the back and the curve on the hood.

7. Finish the hood.

8. Draw the circles for the headlights.

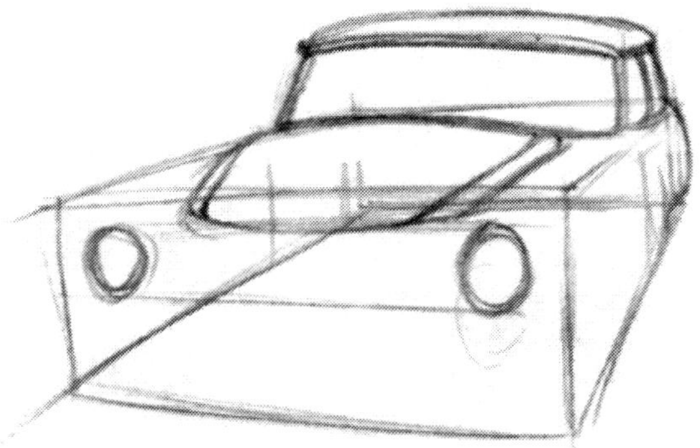

9. Add the rounded line at the rear of the car.

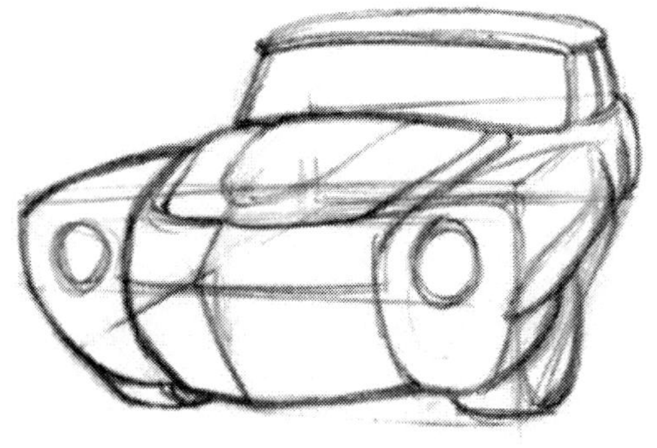

Do not erase the box yet.

10. Add the left front part of the car.

11. Add the tire under the left front fender.

12. Add the right side of the car.

13. Add the tire under the right fender.

14. Add the headlights.

15. Add the rest of the front of the car.

16. Add any missing details to this point.

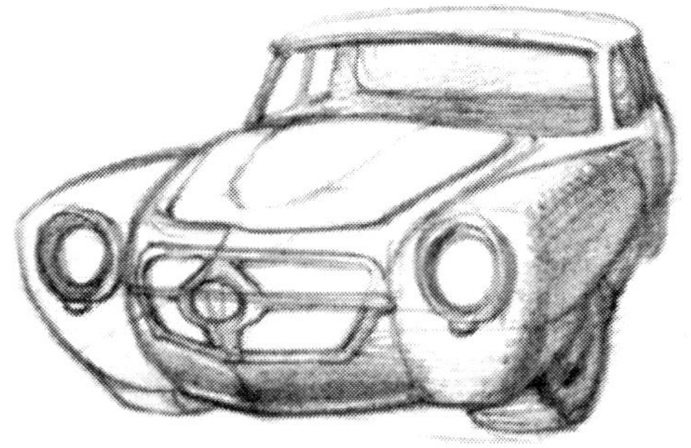

17. Add the details for the inside of the car.

18. Add the details on the front of the car.

19. Detail out the headlights.

20. Add the shading to the car.

21. Erase the guide lines.

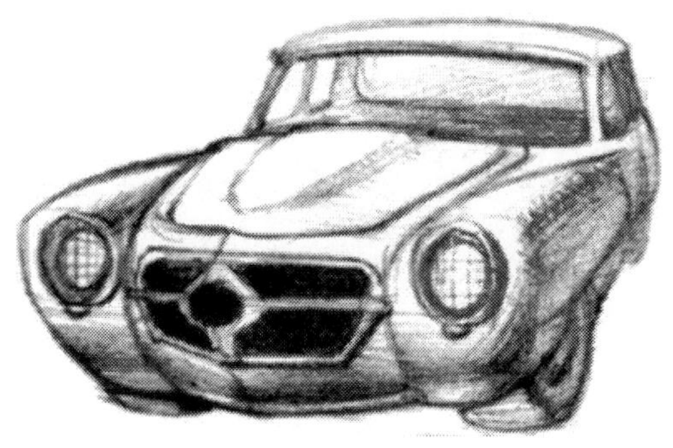

Finish adding all the details you see above to your picture.

Picture 2

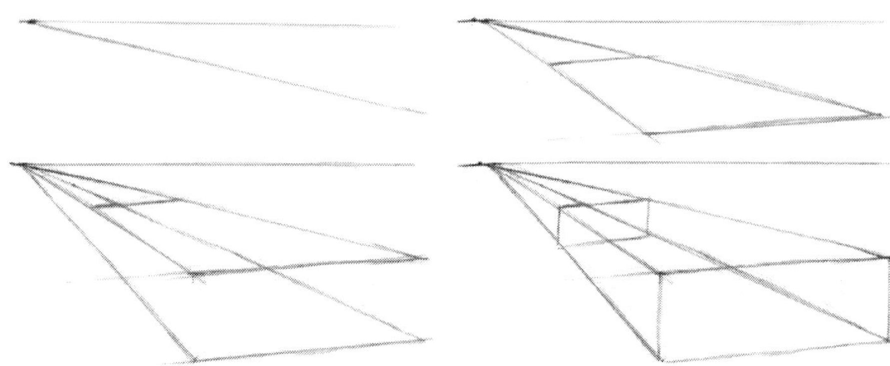

a. Erase the perspective lines.

b. Draw the wheel wells first and then add the curves for the side panel.

c. Draw the other side panel and then the angles for the front. Draw the lines going up to the top of the car's canopy.

d. Add in the canopy.

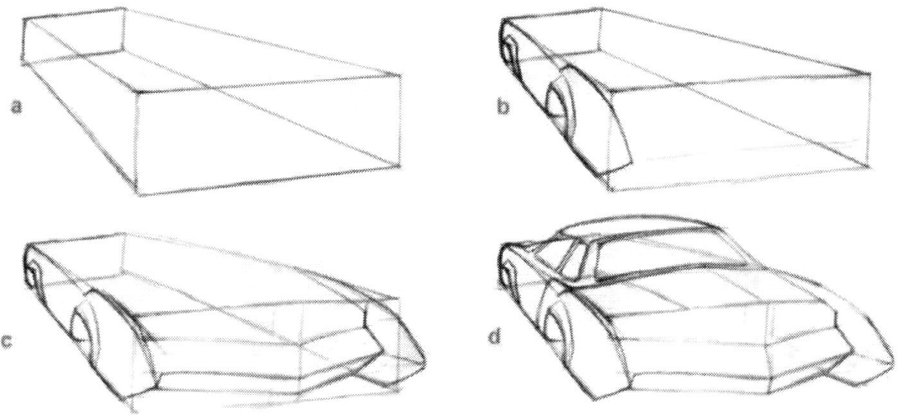

Starting with the top left:

1. Add the rest of the line work to the car. Begin with the front.

2. Don't forget the ornament in the front.

3. Add in the shading as you see it in the following pictures.

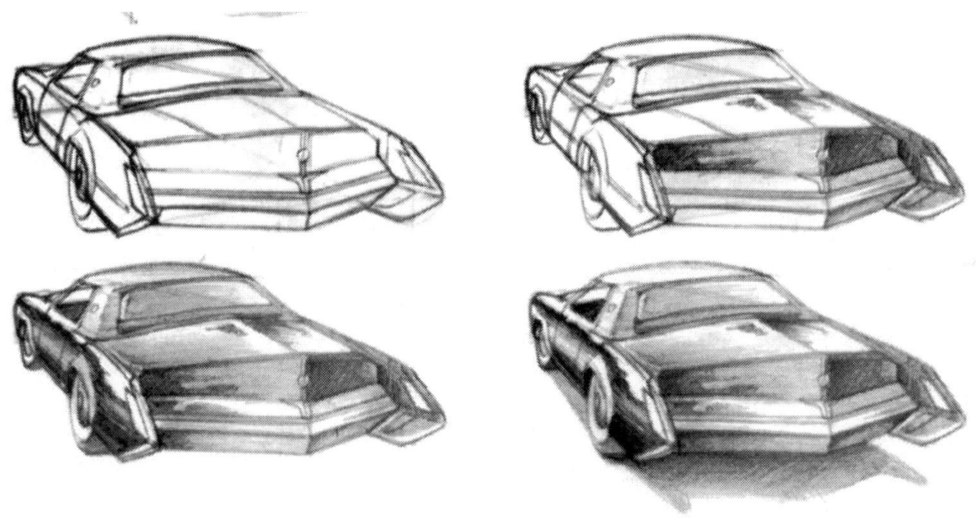

Picture 3

1. Add the starting lines for guides.

2. Finish the 3D rectangle.

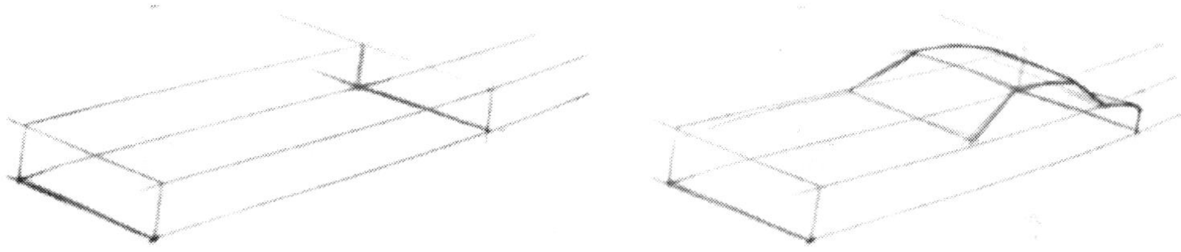

3. Add the top for the canopy.

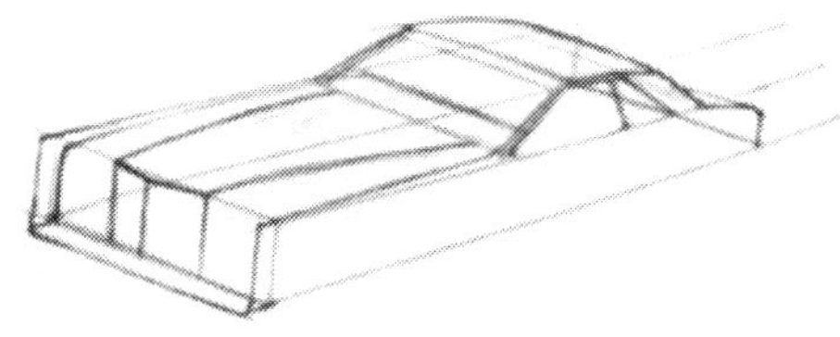

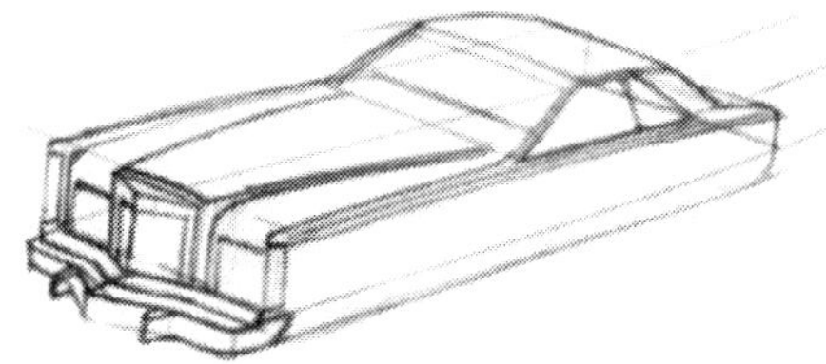

4. Add the detail lines.

5. Add the front bumper and grill.

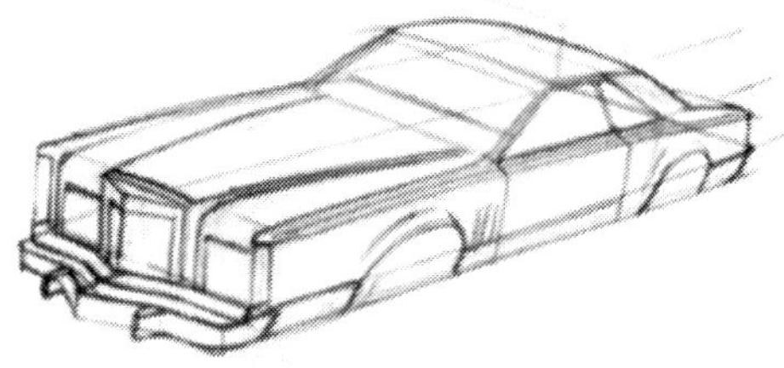

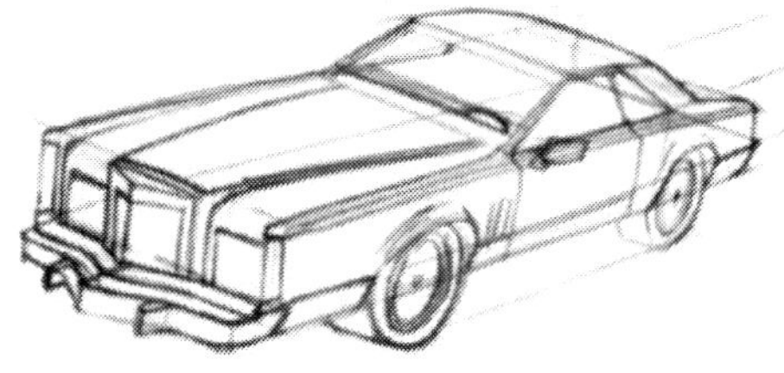

6. Add the side details and the wheel wells.

7.Add the tires.

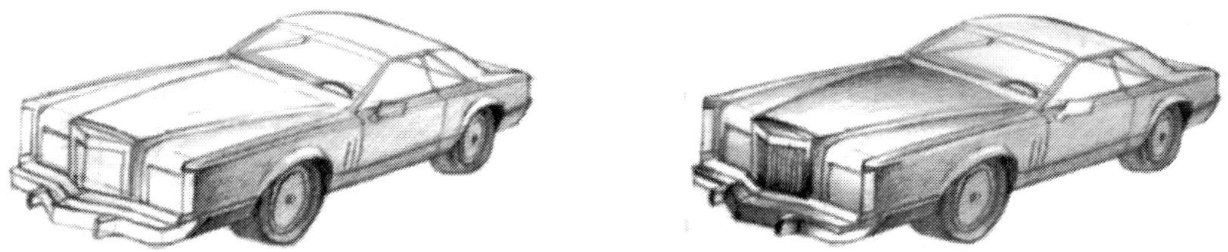

8. Keep adding details.

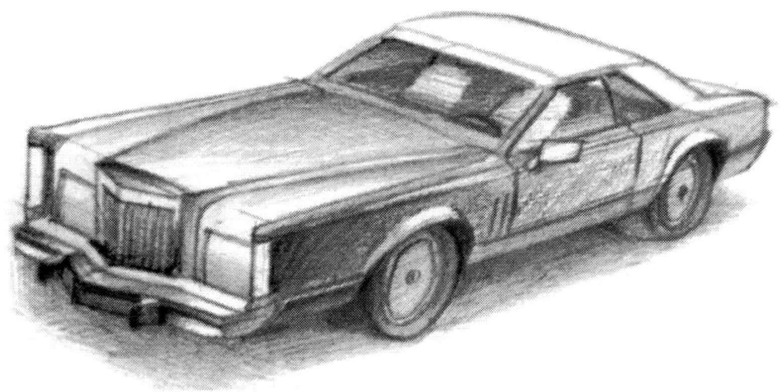

9. Add the shading by using cross hatching.

Chapter 7 – Clothes

One of the hardest things to master drawing is cloth. Here are a few projects to follow.

Fabric

1. Draw the curve first.

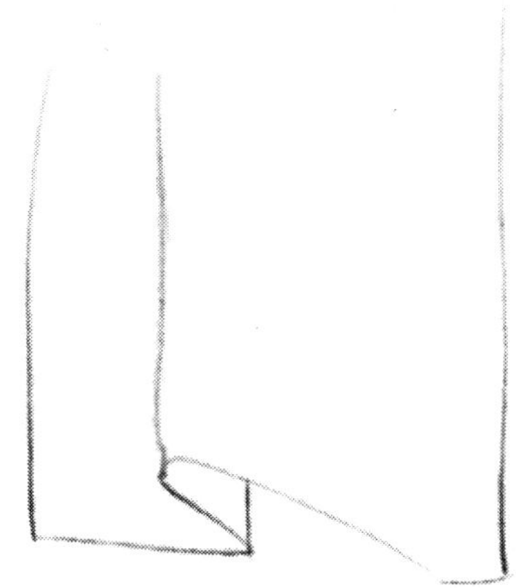

2. Add the lines.

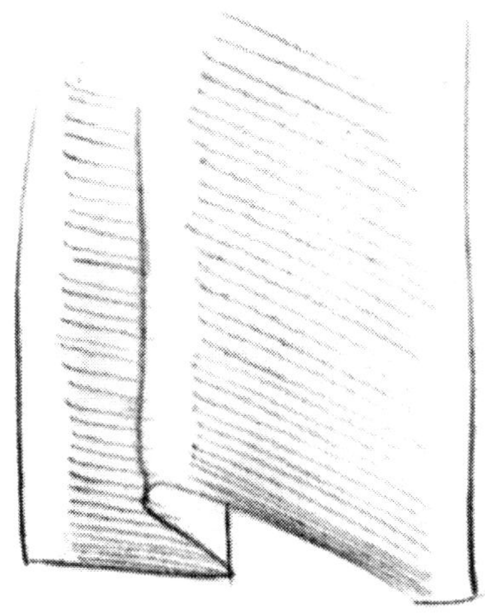

3. Add the hatching lines.

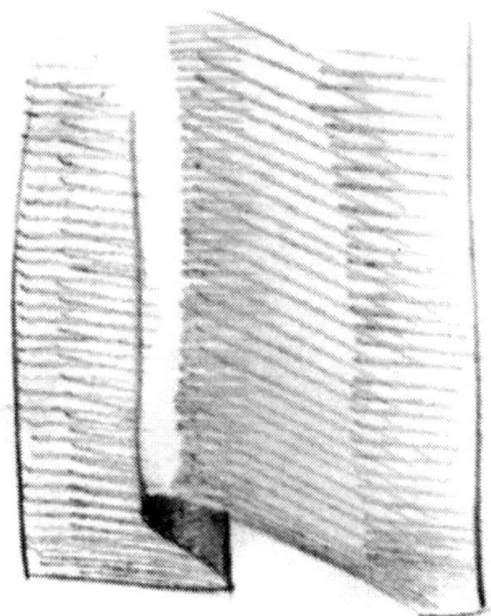

4. Add more hatching lines overlapping the first set.

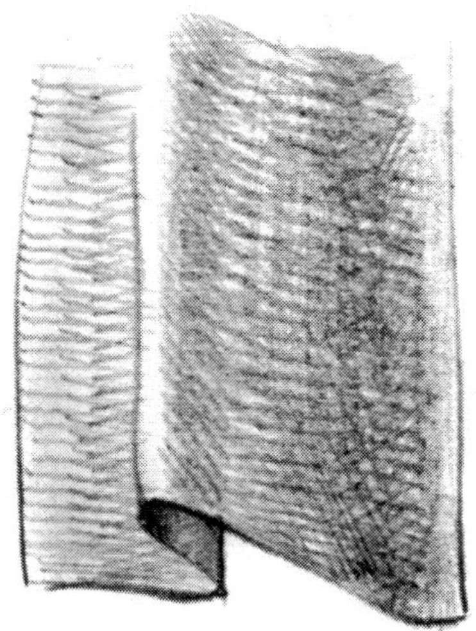

5. Keep hatching until you get the shading.

Draping

1. Add the curved lines first.

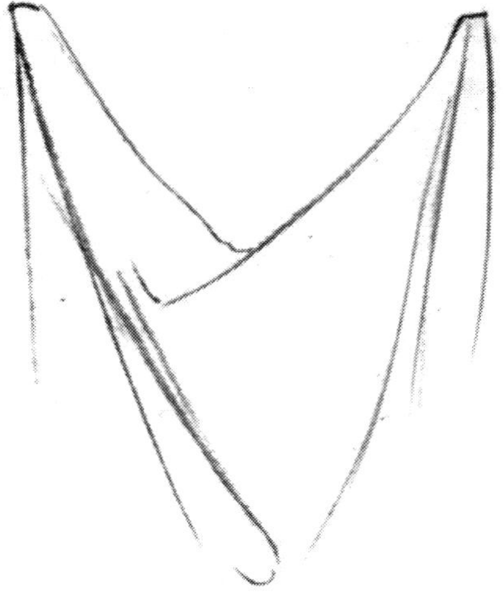

2. Add the lines going down on the sides next.

3. Add the rest of the lines.

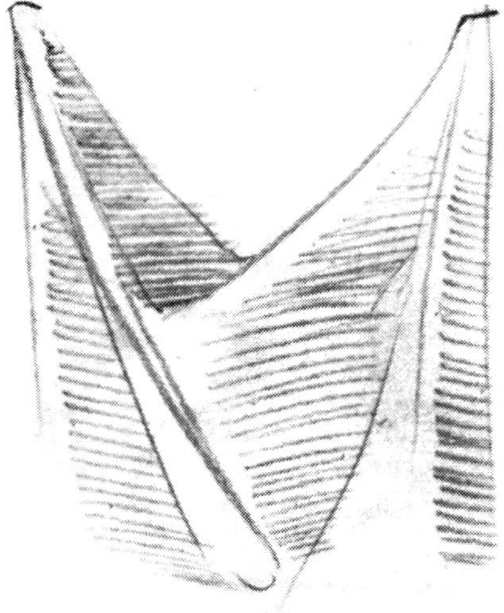

4. Add the hatching lines.

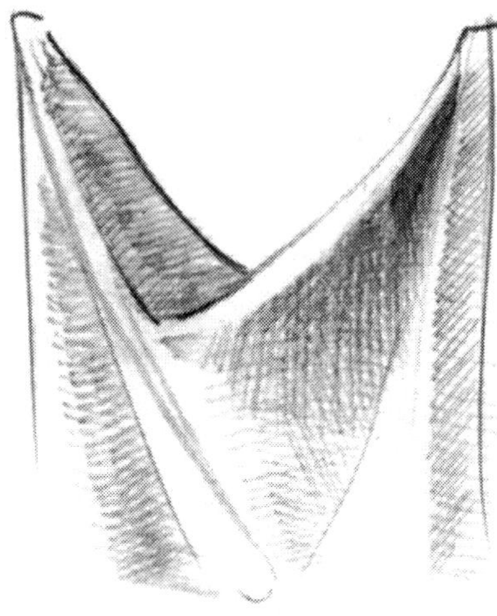

5. Darken the lines on the top of the draping cloth.

6. Use crosses hatching for the shading.

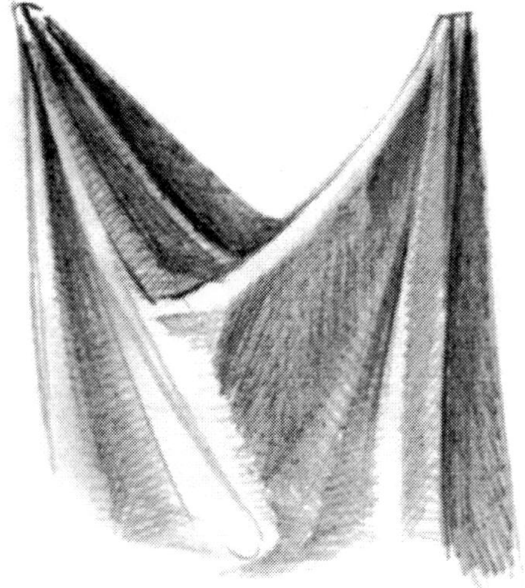

7. Keep darkening the lines until you get the effect on the left.

Advance draping

1. Draw the curved lines.

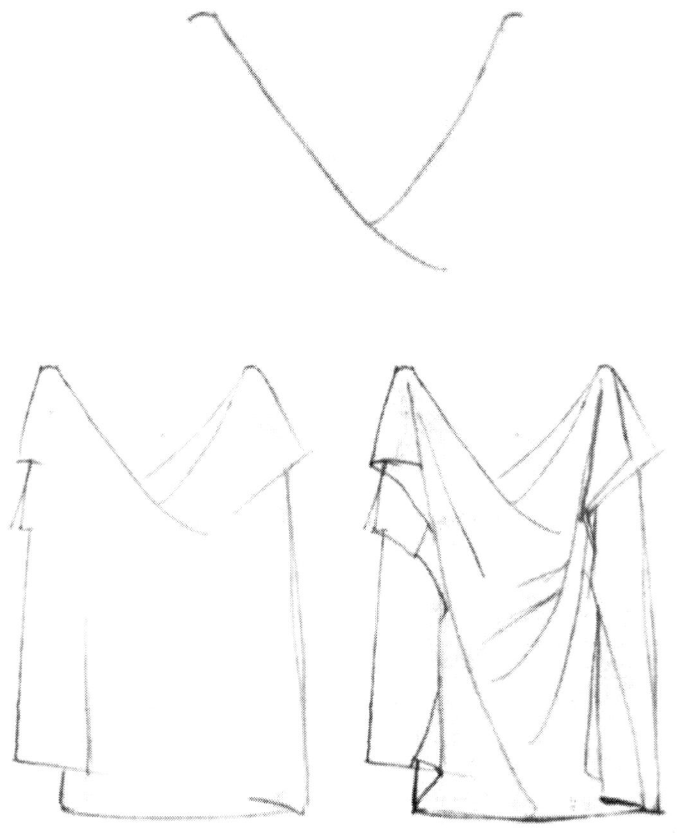

2. On the left, add “L” shapes on the cloth on the far side.

3. Add the lines on the right side of the cloth.

4. Add the lines on the bottom.

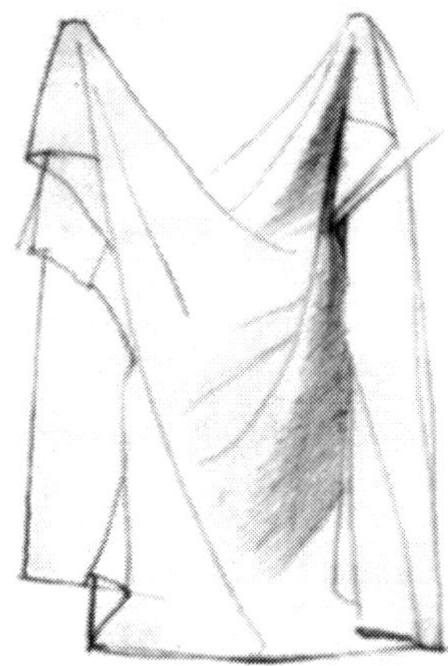

5. Starting from the top, add the lines you see in the diagram on the right.

6. Add the shade on the right side.

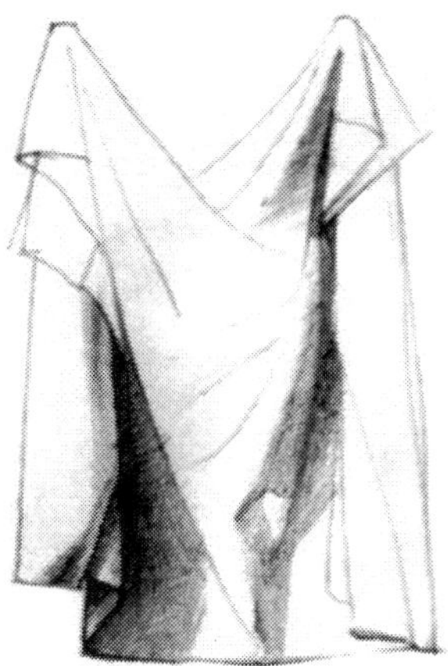

7. Using cross hatching, add the shading on the left side of the cloth.

8. Add more shading on the right side.

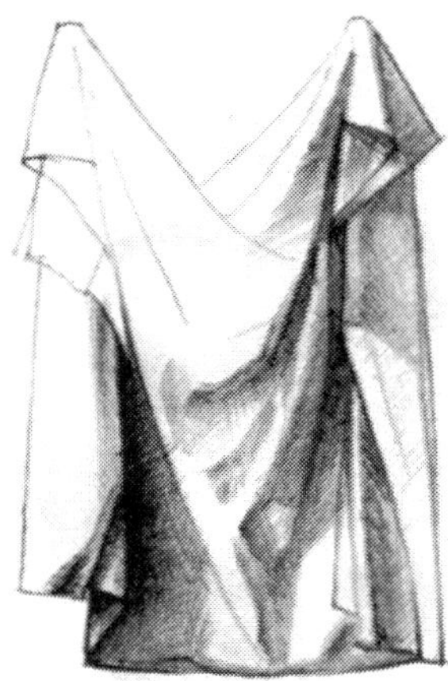

9. Using the lighter lines as a guide, make the shading for the folds in the middle of the cloth.

10. Add the rest of the shading you see in the picture.

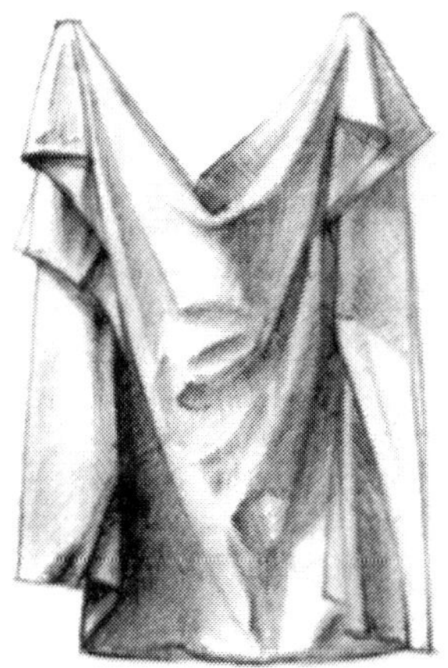

11. Starting at the top of the cloth, shade your way down using cross hatching. Compare what you have with the picture on the left.

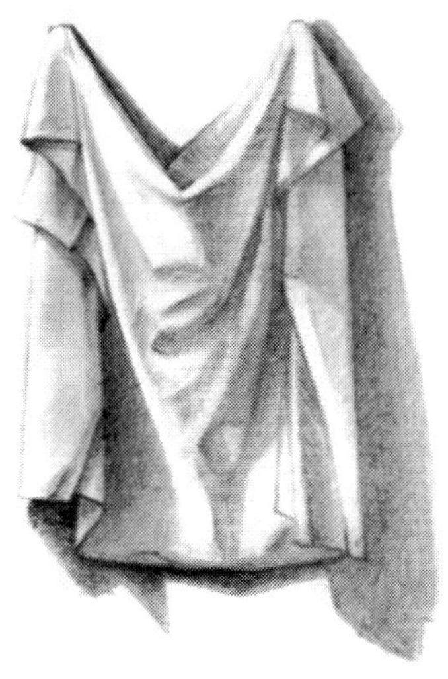

12. Add the shadow behind the cloth.

Extra practice

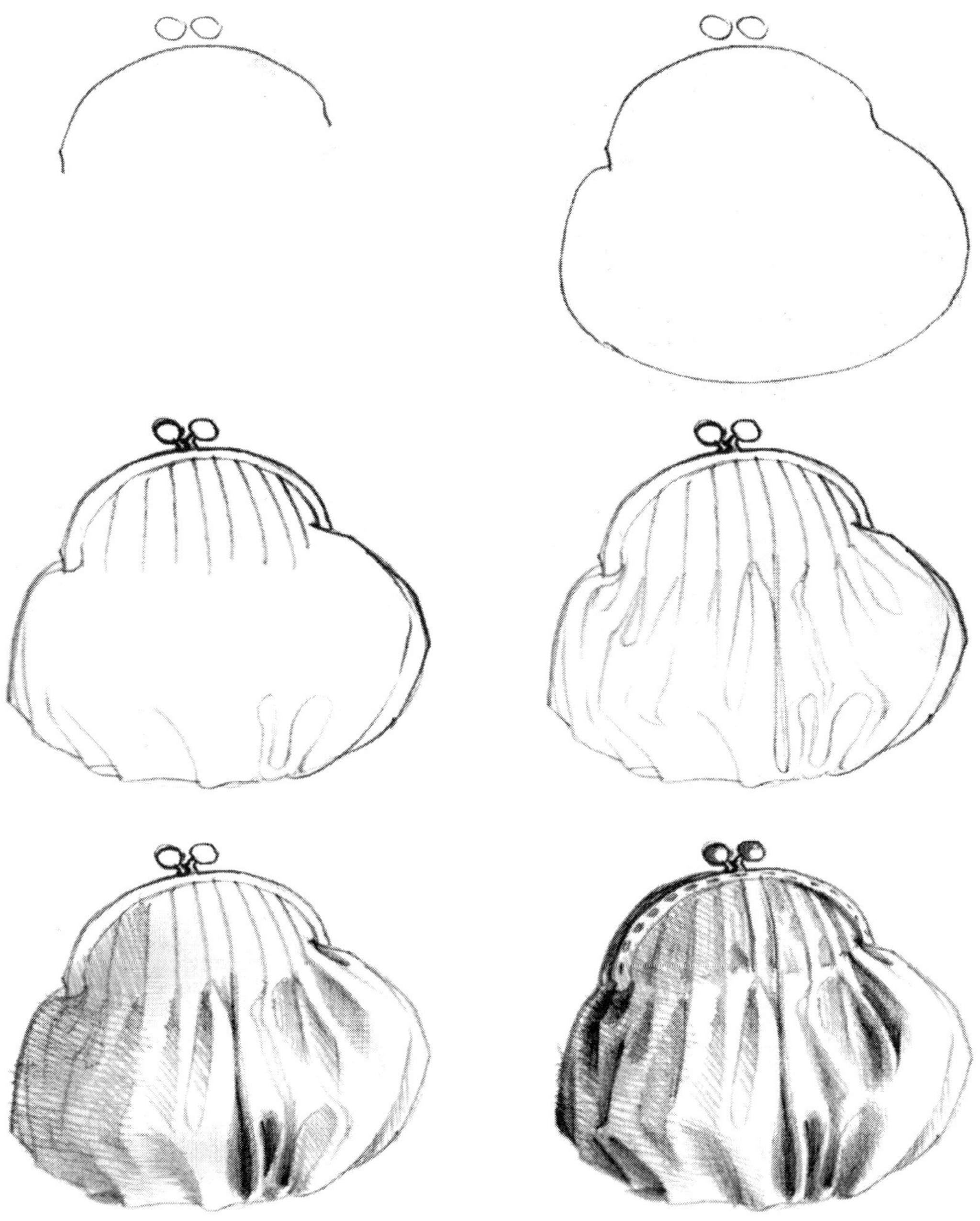

Guess the steps in this project.

Chapter 8 – Animals

The next on the list of subjects to draw are animals. In this chapter, we will cover all types of animals.

Cat

1. Draw the circle.

2. Add rounded triangles for the ears.

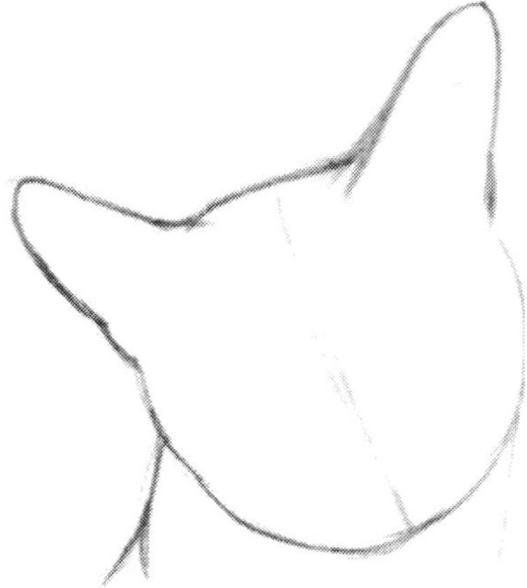

3. Add the nose.

4. Add the curve for the bottom jaw.

5. Draw the curves for the neck.

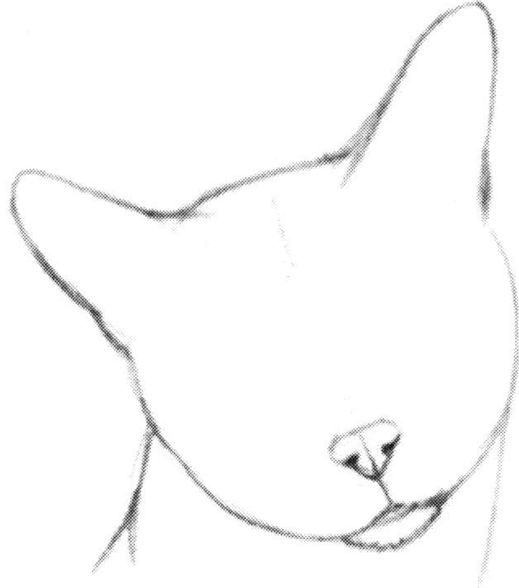

6. Draw the circles for the eyes.

7. Draw the lines for the nose.

8. Shade around the eyes.

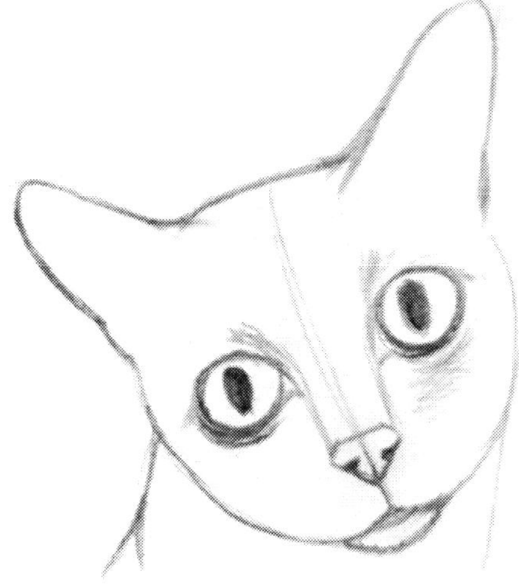

9. Add the pupils for the eyes.

10. Shade inside the ears.

11. Draw the ovals in the eyes.

12. Shade around the ovals in the eyes.

13. Continue shading.

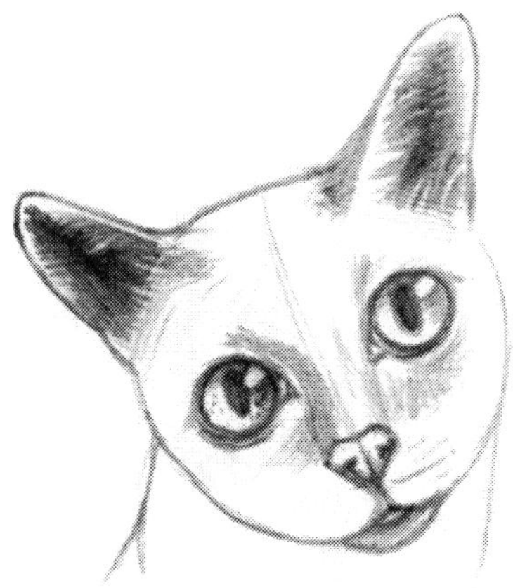

14. Add the whiskers.

15. Finish the shading.

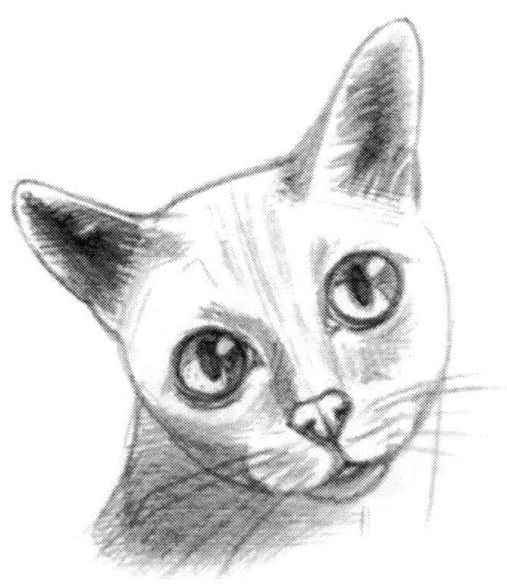

Dog

1. Make the beginning lines you see on the left.

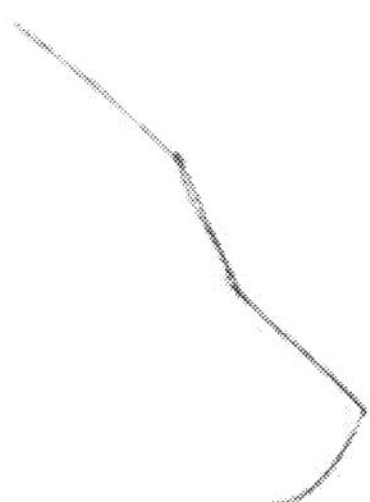

2. Round the snout out a little more.

3. Add the lines for the ear.

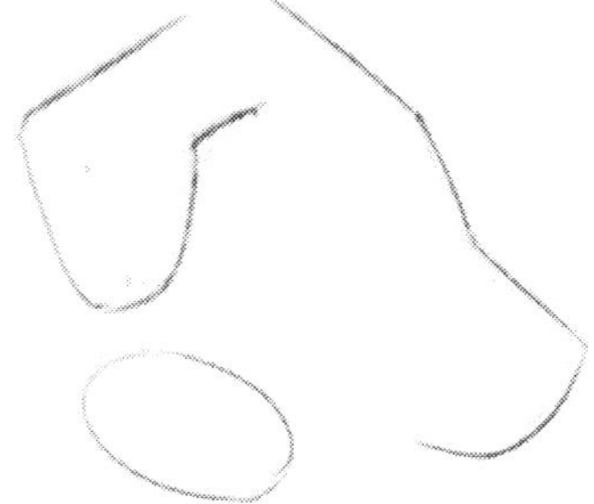

4. Draw the oval on the bottom left.

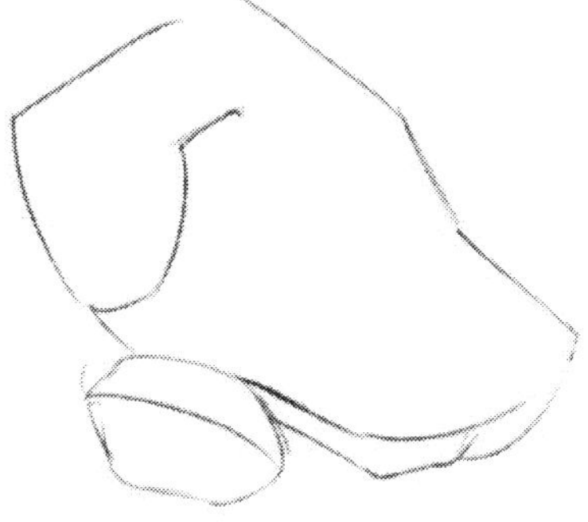

5. Reshape the oval to look a little more like a paw.

6. Draw the lines coming from the paw for the bottom jaw.

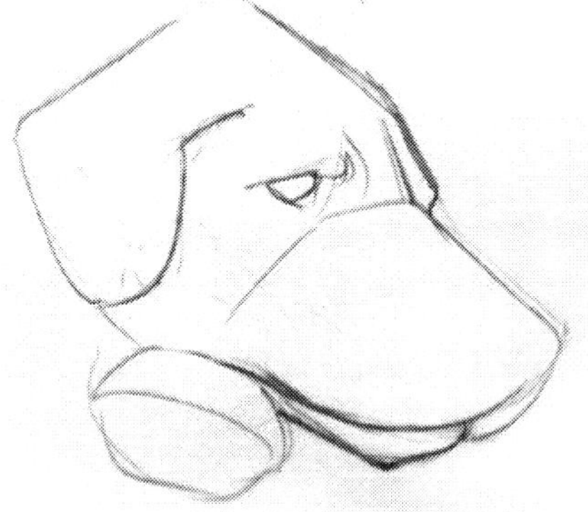

7. Draw the line going to the ear.

8. Add the detail for the snout.

9. Add the eye and its details.

10. Add the details for the forehead.

11. Darken in the mouth.

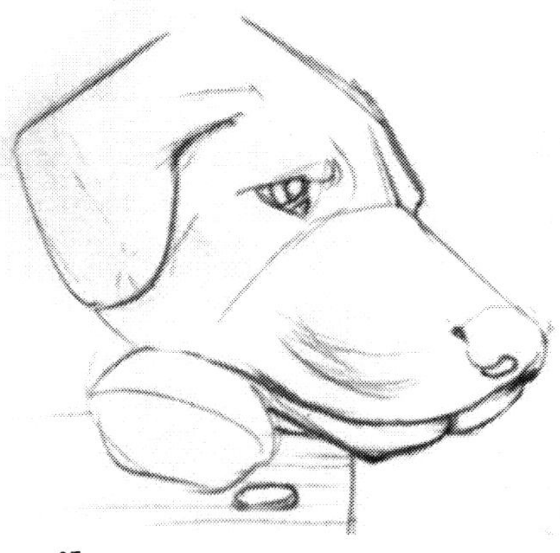

12. Add in the eye details.

13. Add the lines for the nose.

14. Add the whiskers.

15 Add the line for the table.

16. Add any missing details.

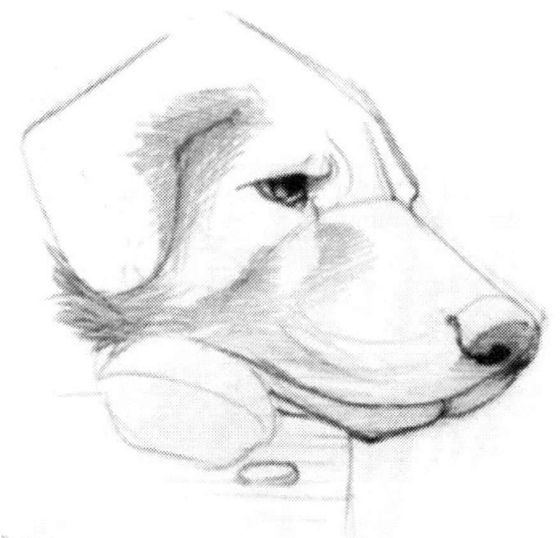

17. Darken in the eye.

18. Add the shading for the fur under the ear.

19. Add the other shading.

20 Add the details for the nose and snout.

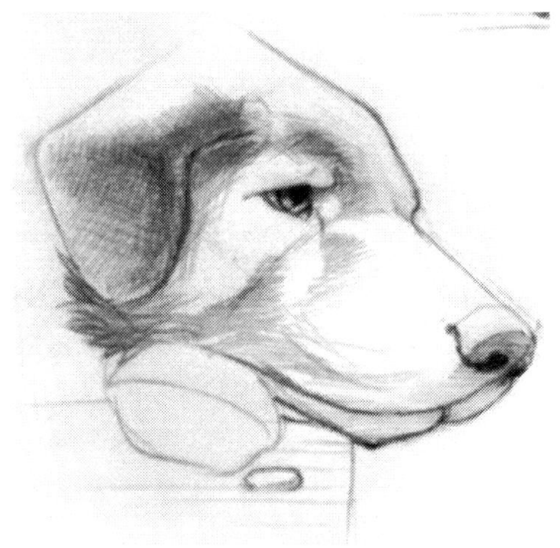

21. Continue to detail and shade.

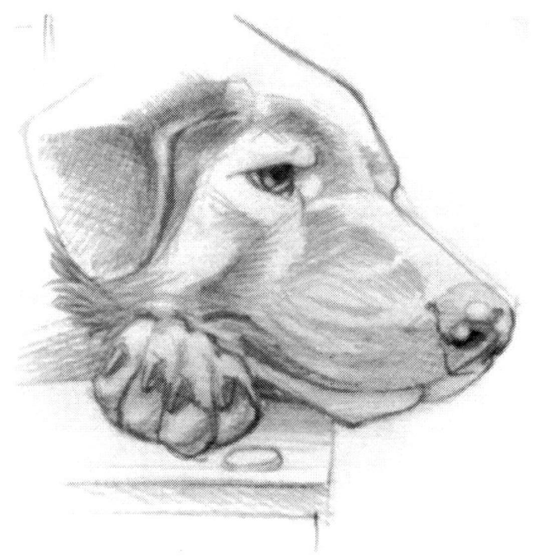

22. Add the lines for the paw separation.

23. Add in the claws.

24. Finish out the shading.

Hedgehog

1. Draw the oval in the picture.

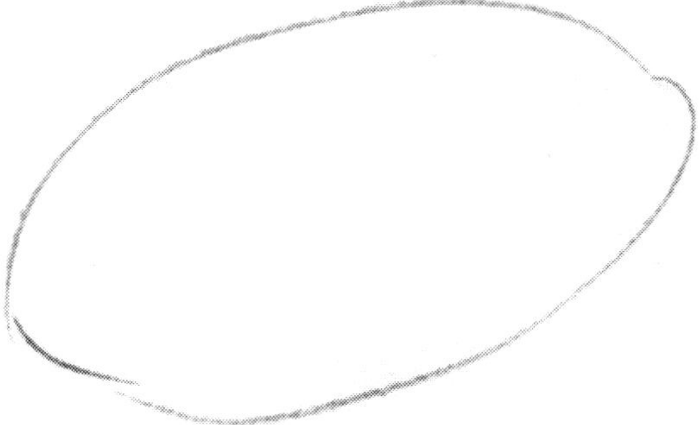

2. Add the bowl shaped curved under the oval.

3. Add the legs.

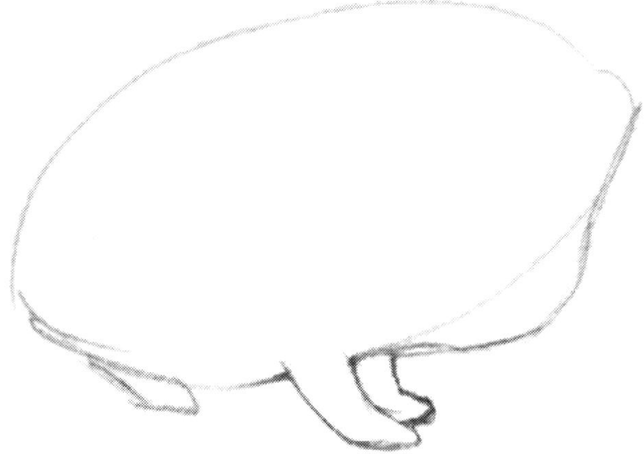

4. Add the lines on the bottom left.

5. Add hash marks for the hedgehog.

6. Add the dots for the eyes and nose.

7. Add the mouth.

8. Add the ears.

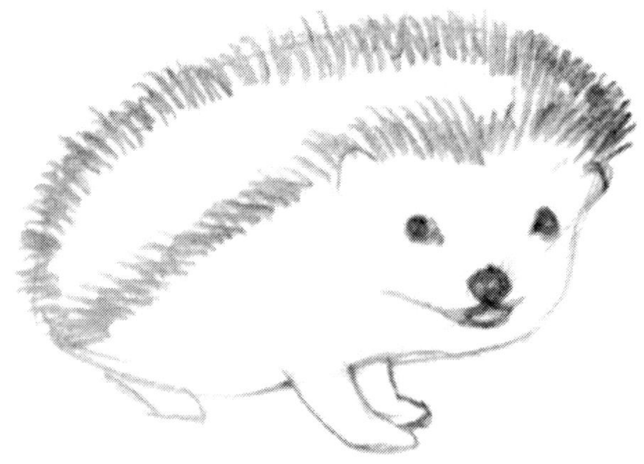

9. Add the rest of the quills.

10. Darken the ears.

11. Add the rest of the details.

12. Finish the shading.

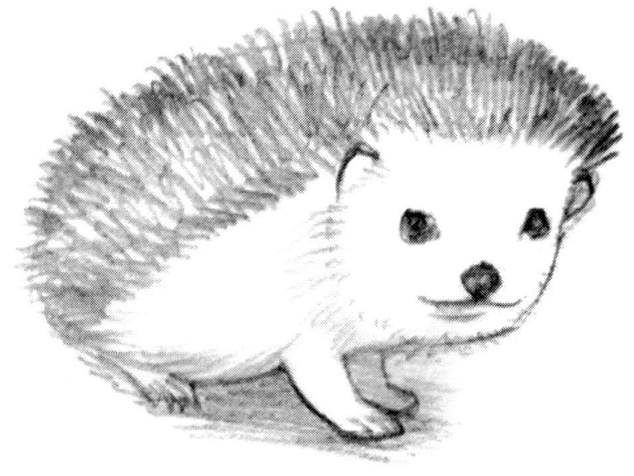

Snake

1. Draw the line you see in the picture.

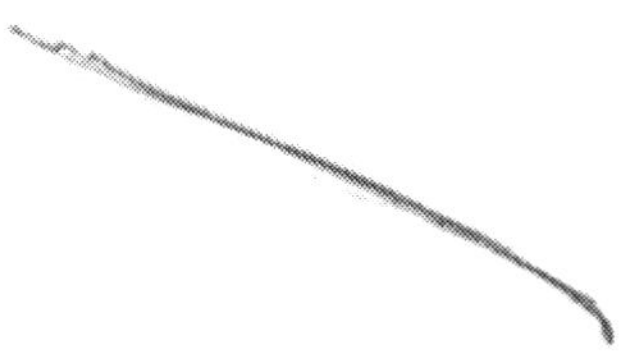

2. Draw the cross line.

3. Add the circles.

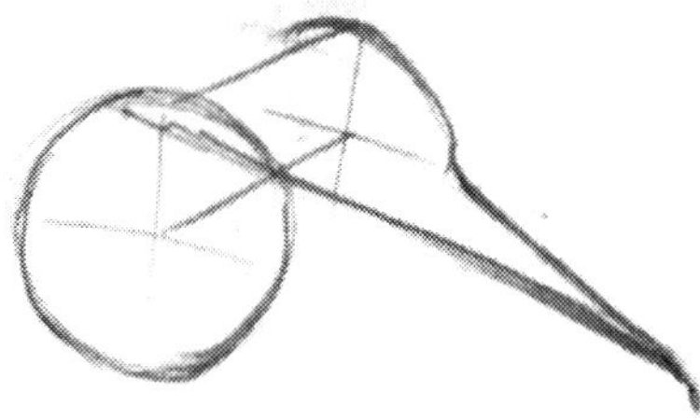

4. Add the dark shading behind the head.

5. Draw the line in the back.

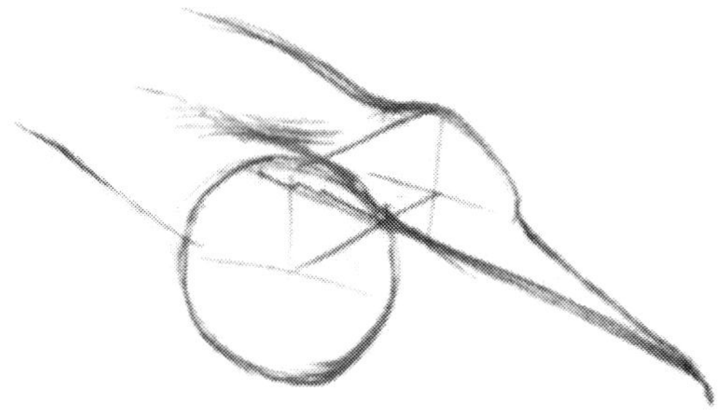

6. Draw the inside of the eye.

7. Draw the line for the nose of the snake.

8. Draw the line from the eye to the back of the head.

9. Draw the line under eye.

10. Finish out the head on the far side of the picture.

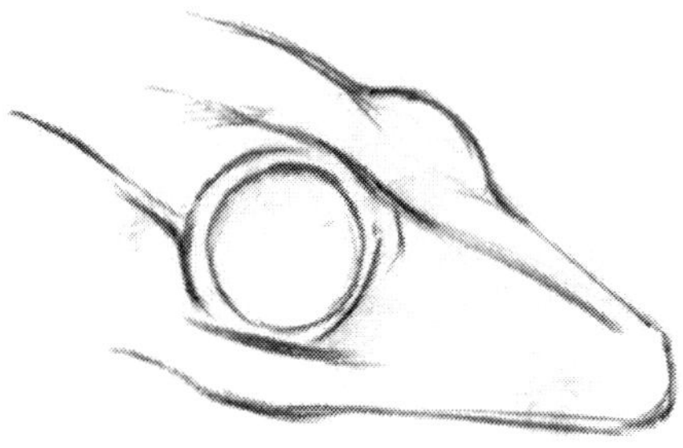

11. Add the top of the lower jaw.

12. Add the jaw details.

13. Add the lines for the neck.

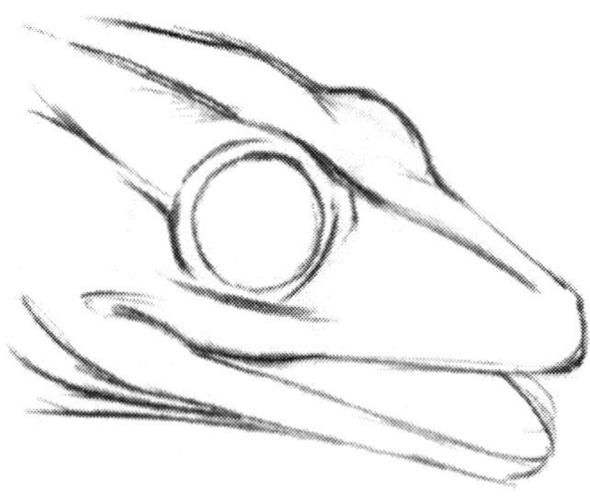

14. Add the inside of the eye.

15. Add the hatch marks for the scales.

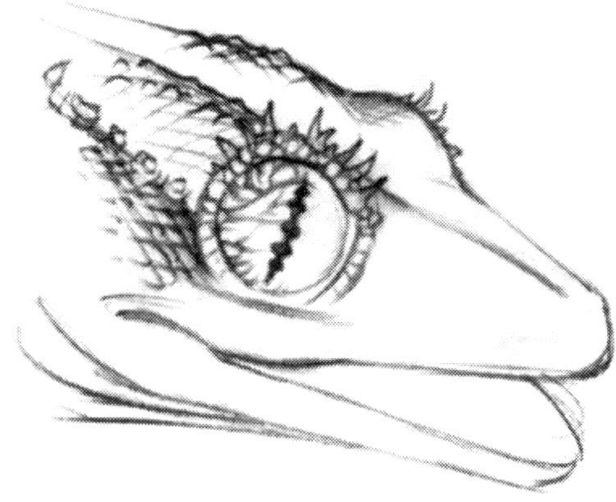

Take this time to double check to make sure you haven't left anything out.

16. Draw the line to snub the nose.

17. Shade the snub of the nose.

18. Add the rest of the scales.

19. Add the shading you see in the picture.

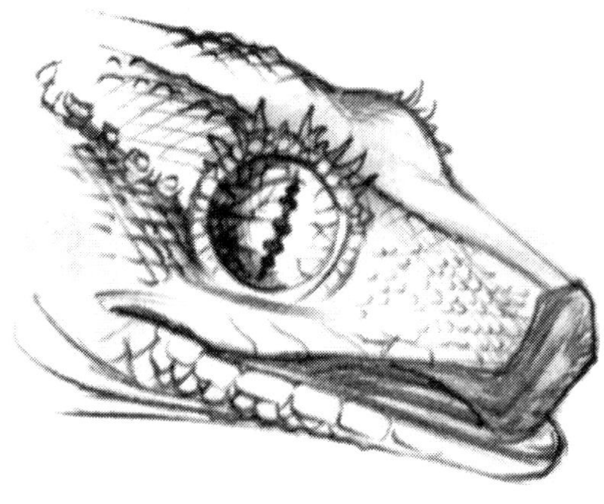

Fox

1. Add the trapezoid.

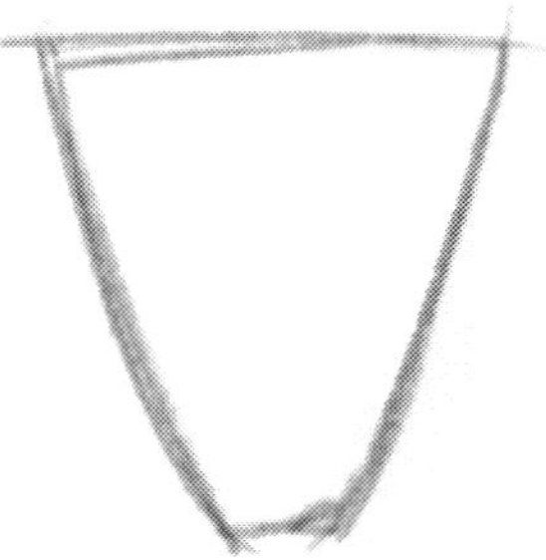

2. Draw in the rectangle under the first shape.

3. Draw the line going down the middle.

4. Draw the elongated "D" shape for the body.

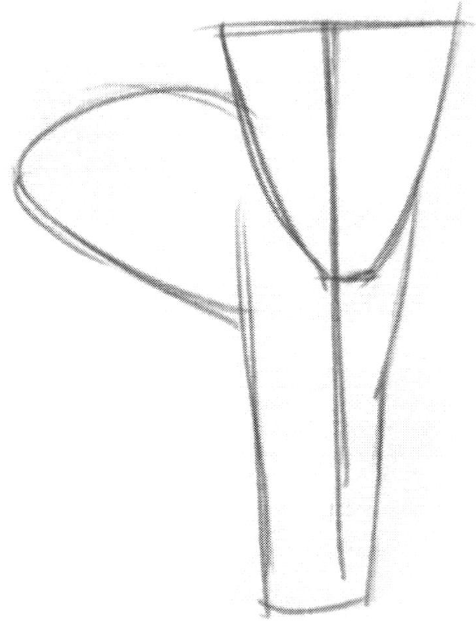

5. Draw the rectangle under the body for the rear legs.

6. Draw the start of the tail.

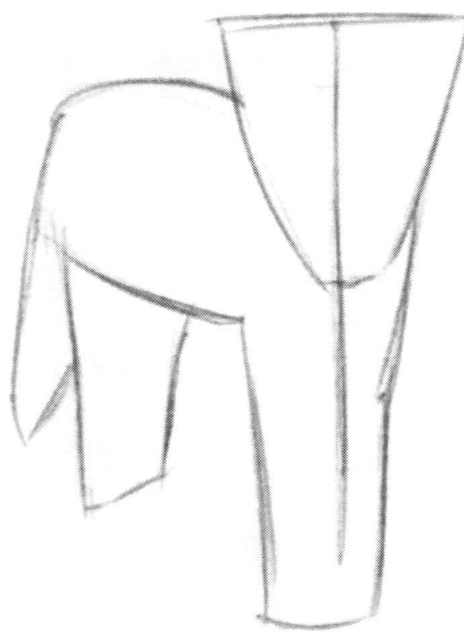

7. Using the bisecting line, draw upside-down “U”s for the ears and one for the front of the fox.

8. Add the lines for the claws.

9. Add a little bit of detail.

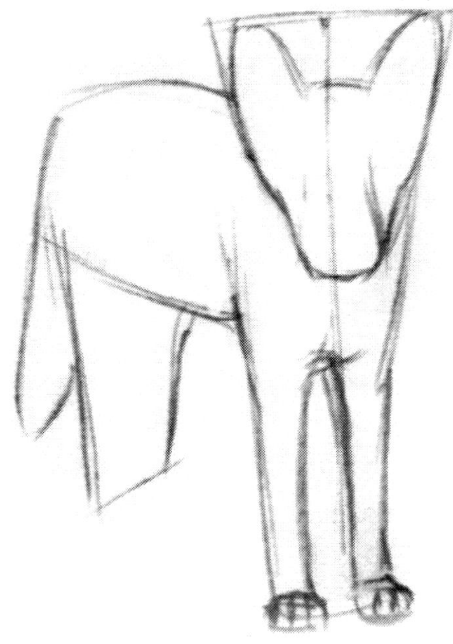

9. Shade in the ears.

10. Draw the tear drops for the eyes.

11. Add the pupils.

12. Add the nose.

13. Shade around the face.

14. Shade the front of the legs.

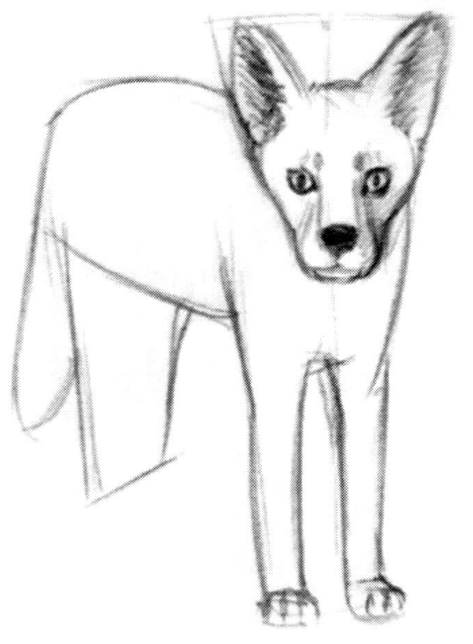

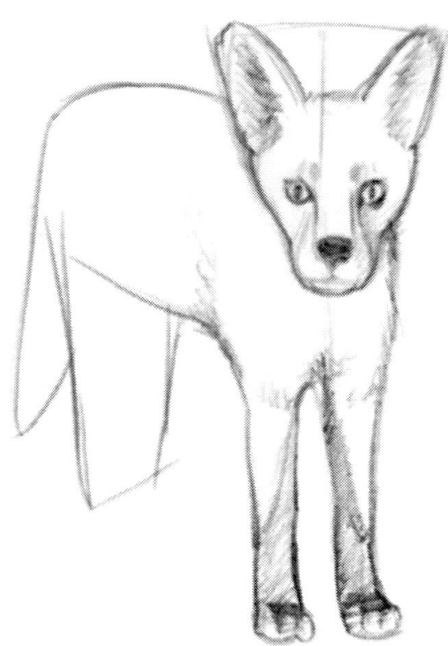

15. Starting from the left, add the shading until you get the effects above.

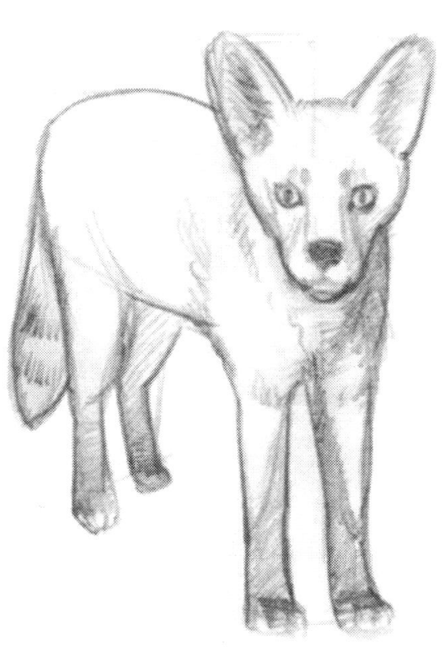

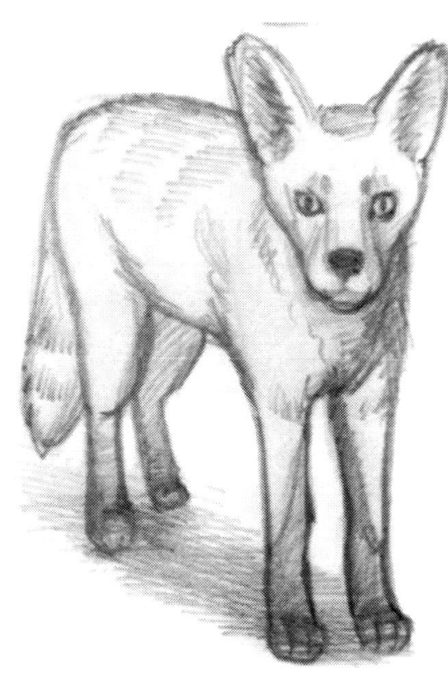

Bird

1. Draw the sideways “L” shape.

2. Add the fan shape.

3. Round out the body.

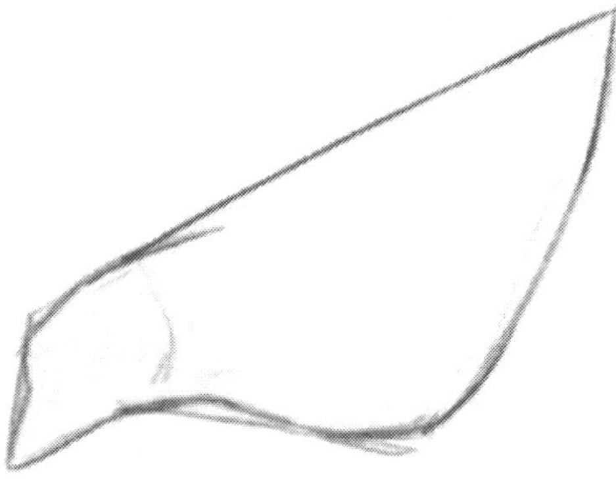

4. Add the beak.

5. Draw the dot for the eye and then the details for the eye.

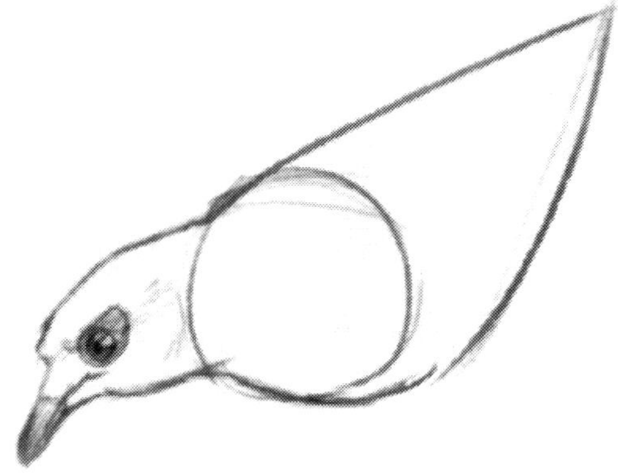

6. Make the body into a tear drop.

7. Add the tail.

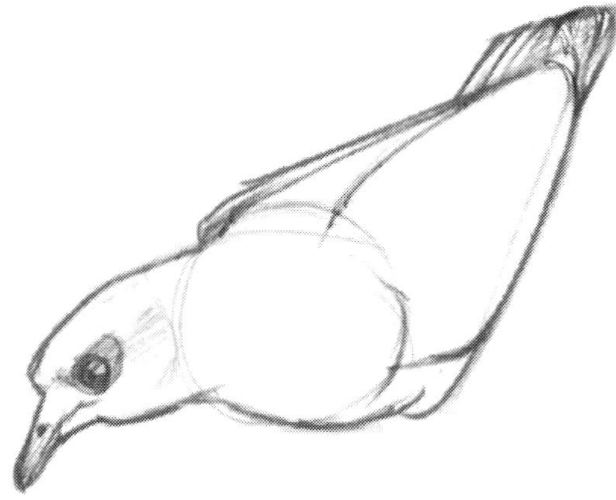

8. Compare and add the details you haven't yet.

9. Add the details for the wing and tail.

11. Draw the legs.

12. Add the branch.

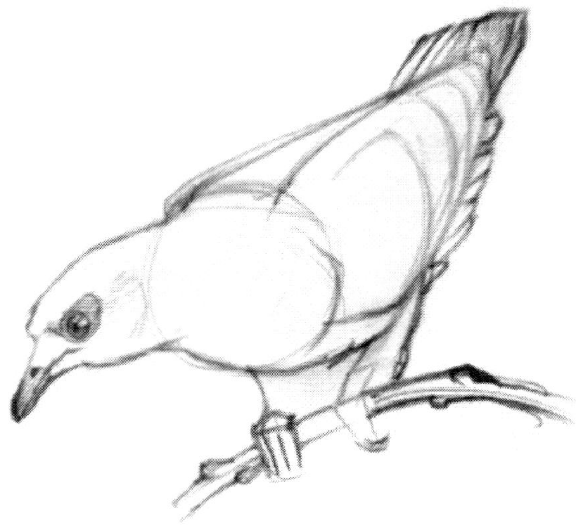

13. Use a series of bumps for the rear of the bird.

14. Add the details for the claws.

15. Add the accents for the feathers.

16. Add the shading.

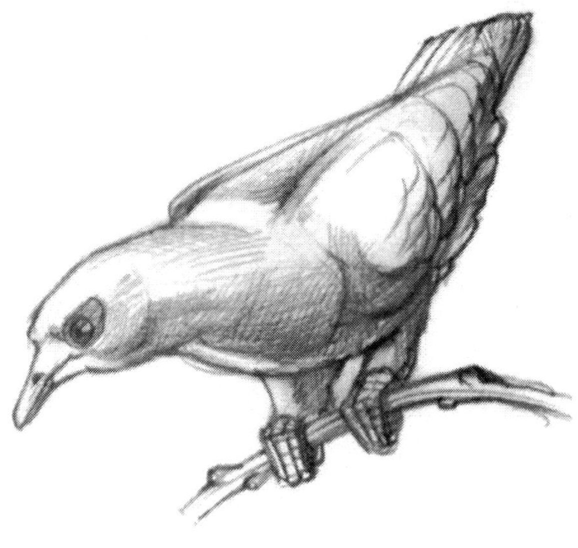

Deer

1. Draw a wide "V" for the top of the head.

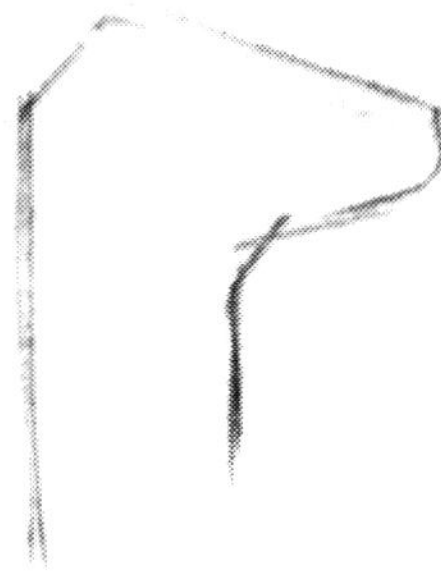

2. Add a curve for the muzzle.

3. Draw the straight lines for the neck.

4. Draw 2 "L" shapes for the body.

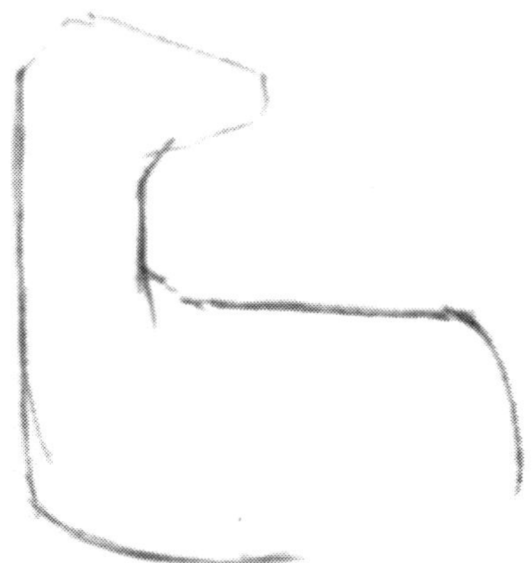

5. Draw the lines for the legs above. Take your time.

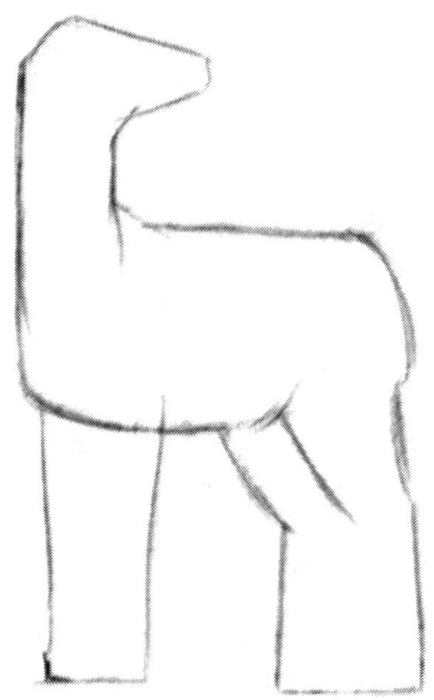

6. Add the line for the leg gap.

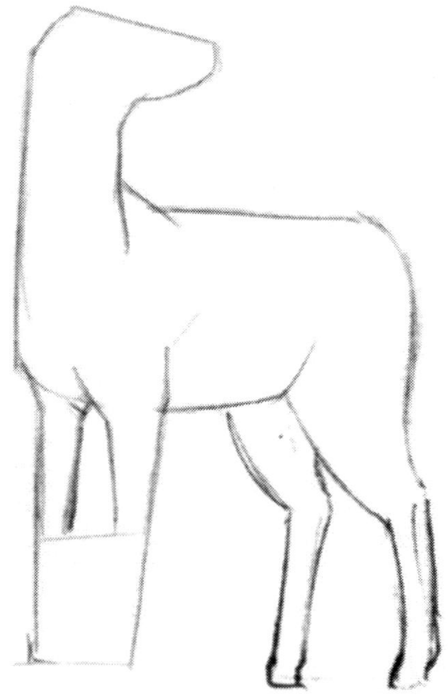

7. Draw the spaces for the front and back.

8. Add the squared-off hooves.

9. Add the "V" for the ear.

10. Add the dot for the eye.

11. Add the line for the mouth.

12. Add the shading for the nose.

13. Add the accents for the neck, legs and other parts of the body.

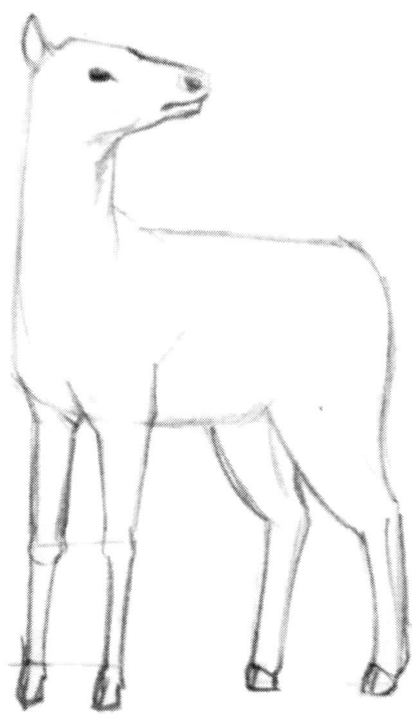

14. Draw in the antlers.

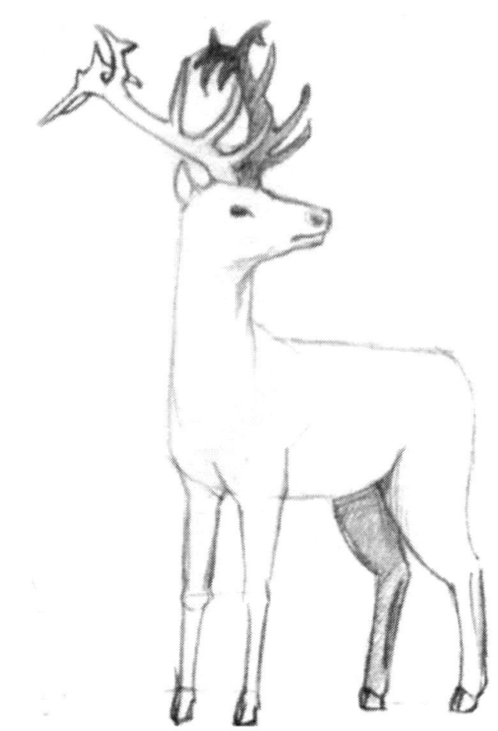

15. Shade the picture in.

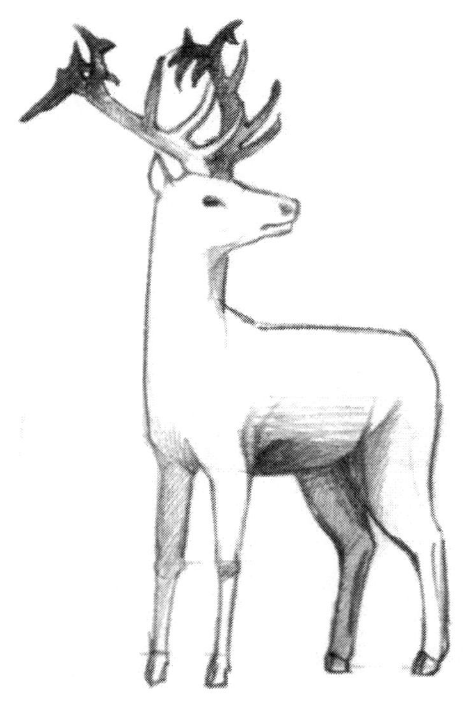

Extra practice

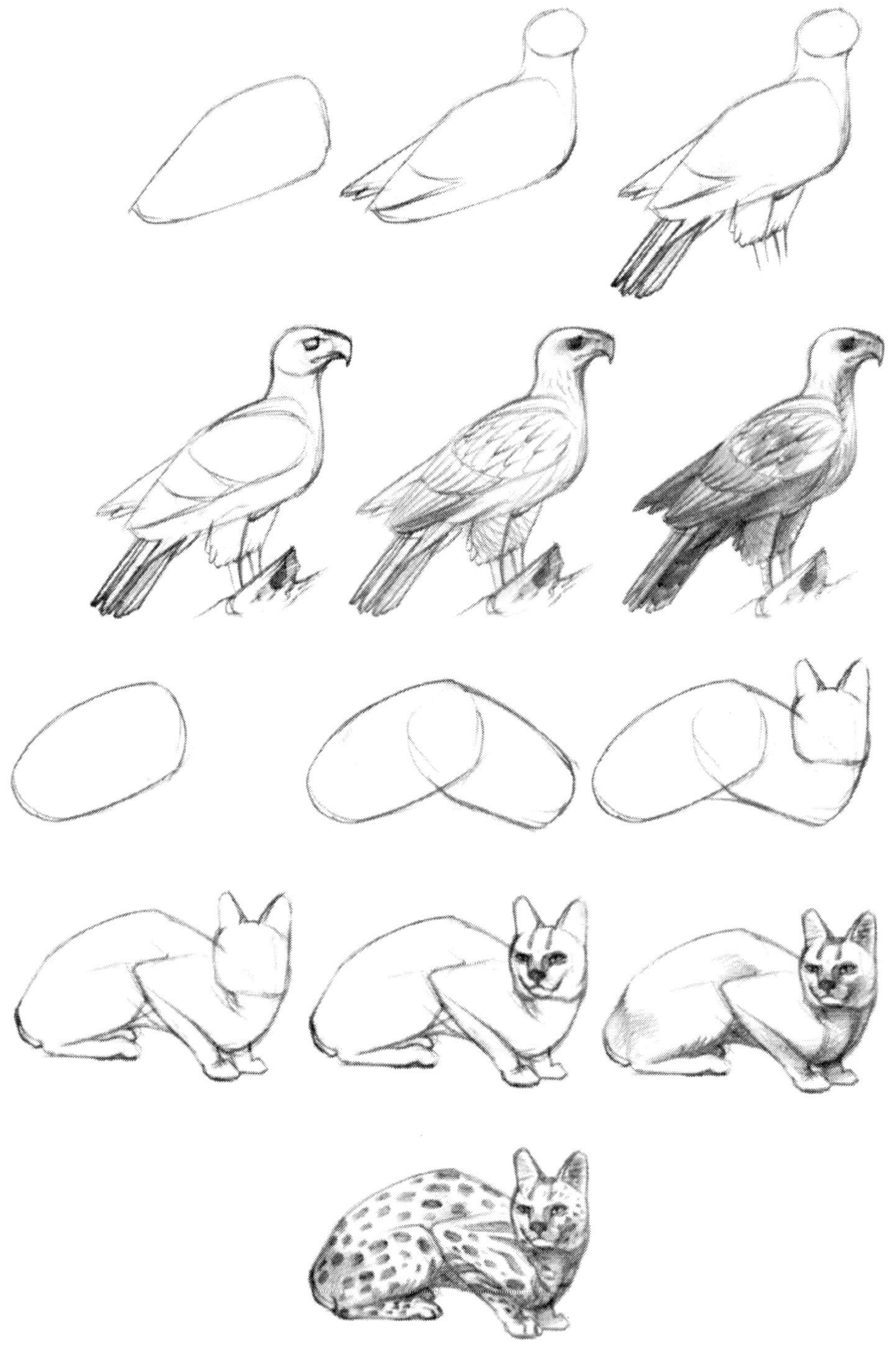

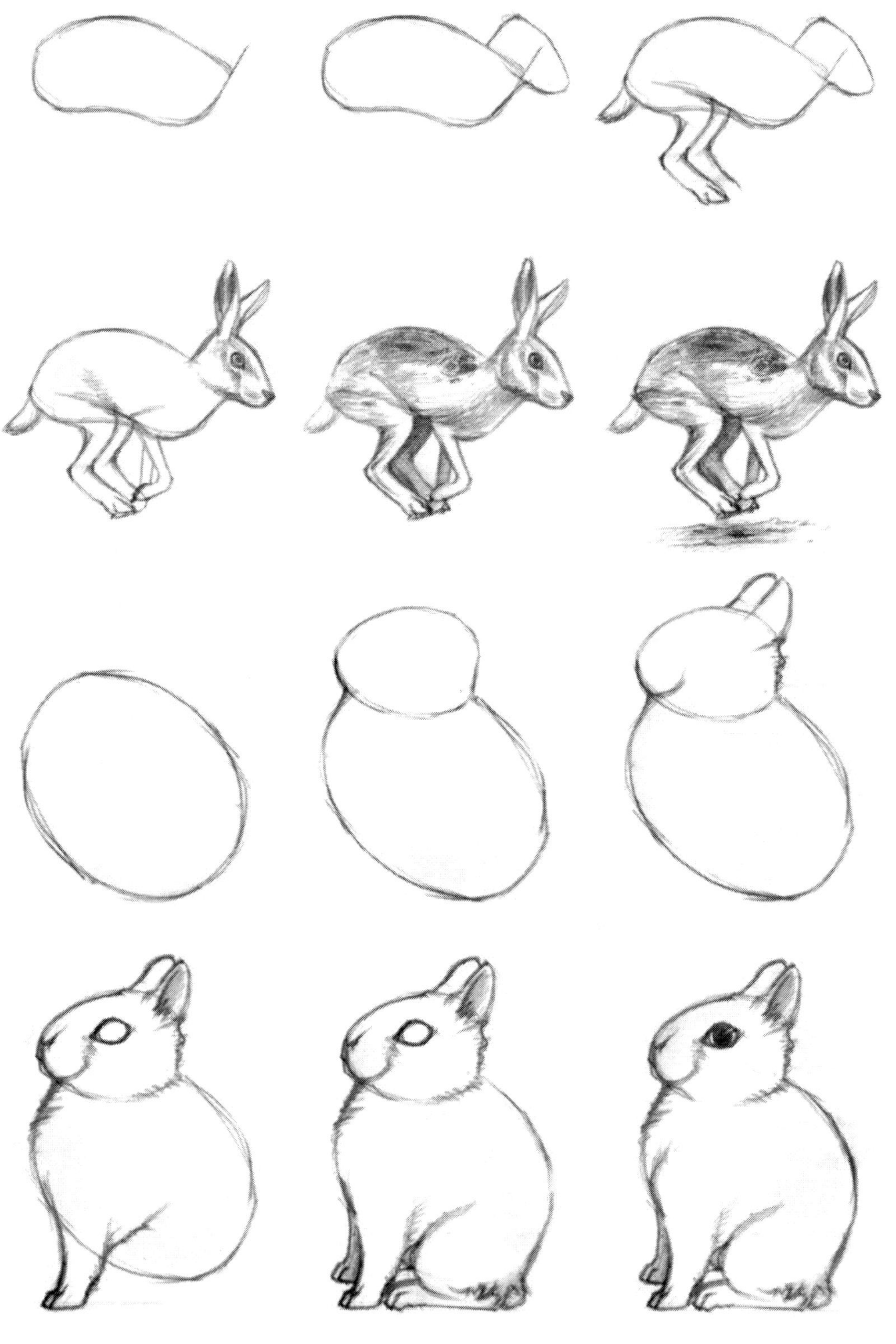

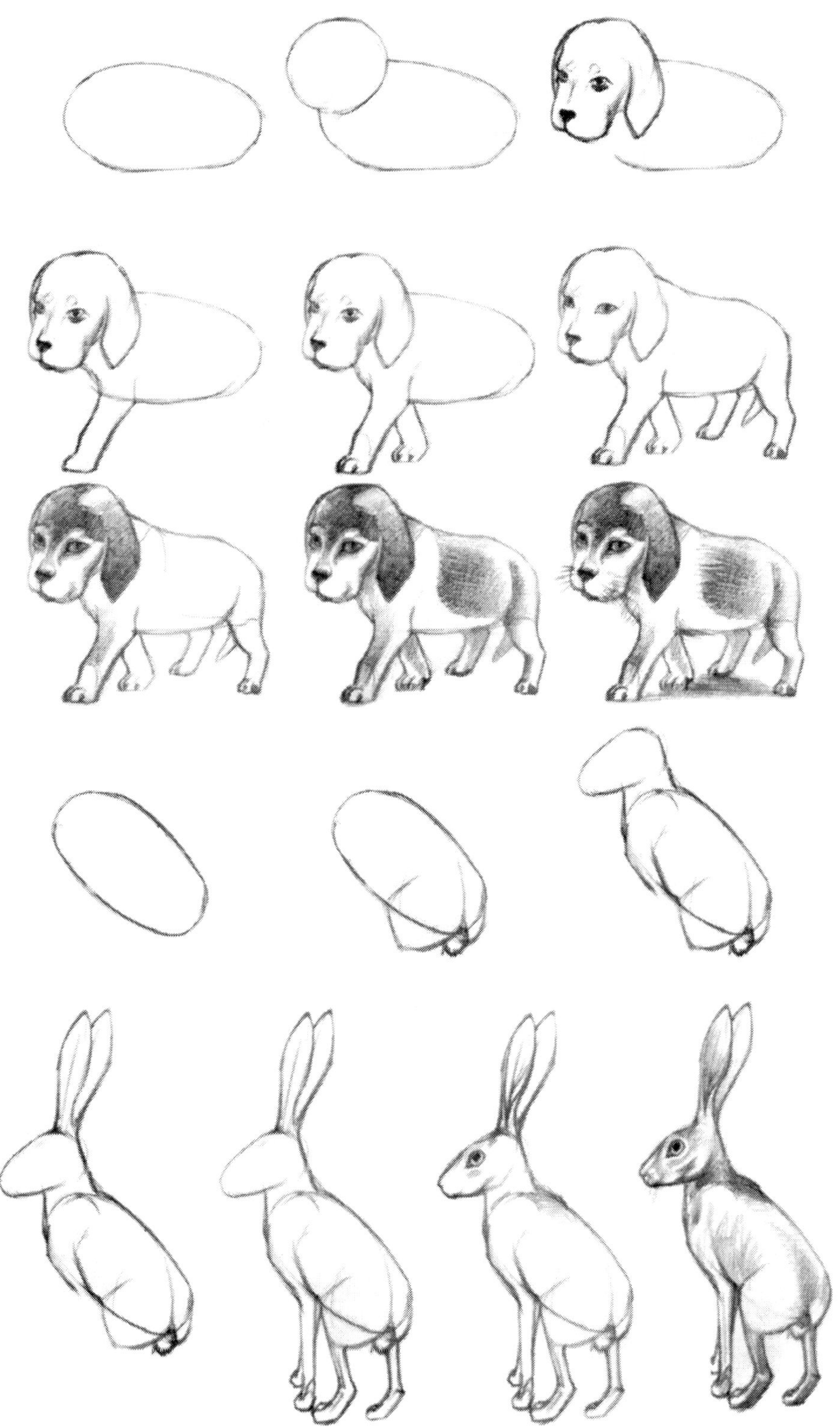

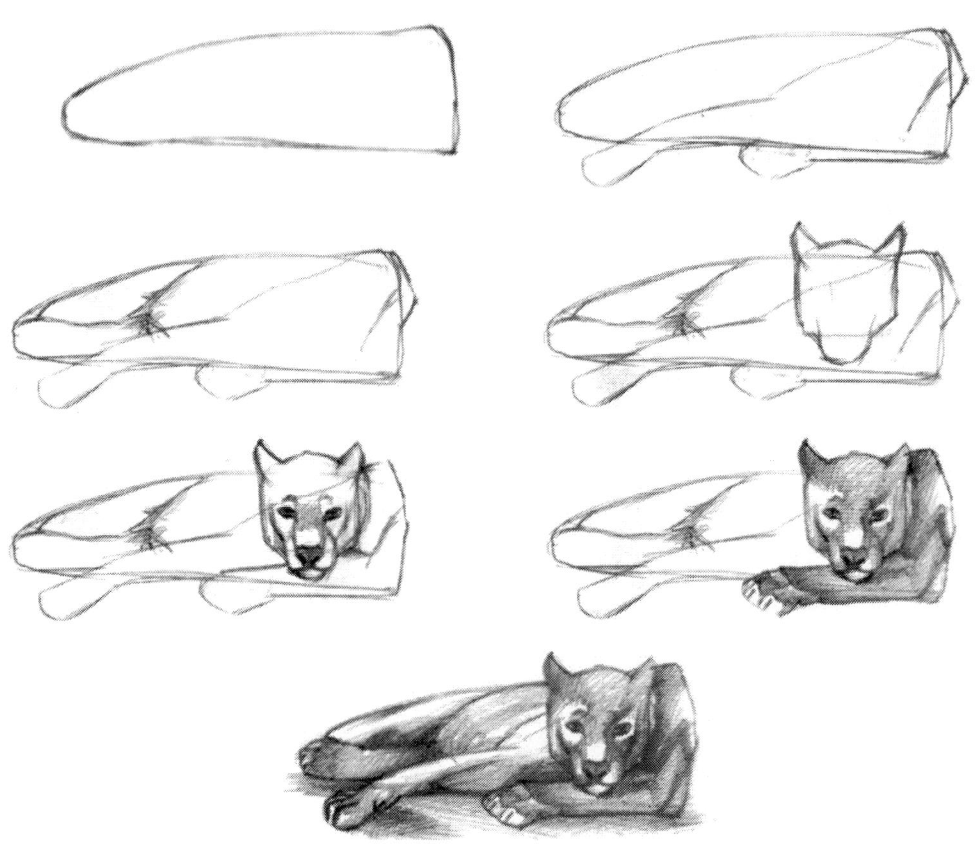

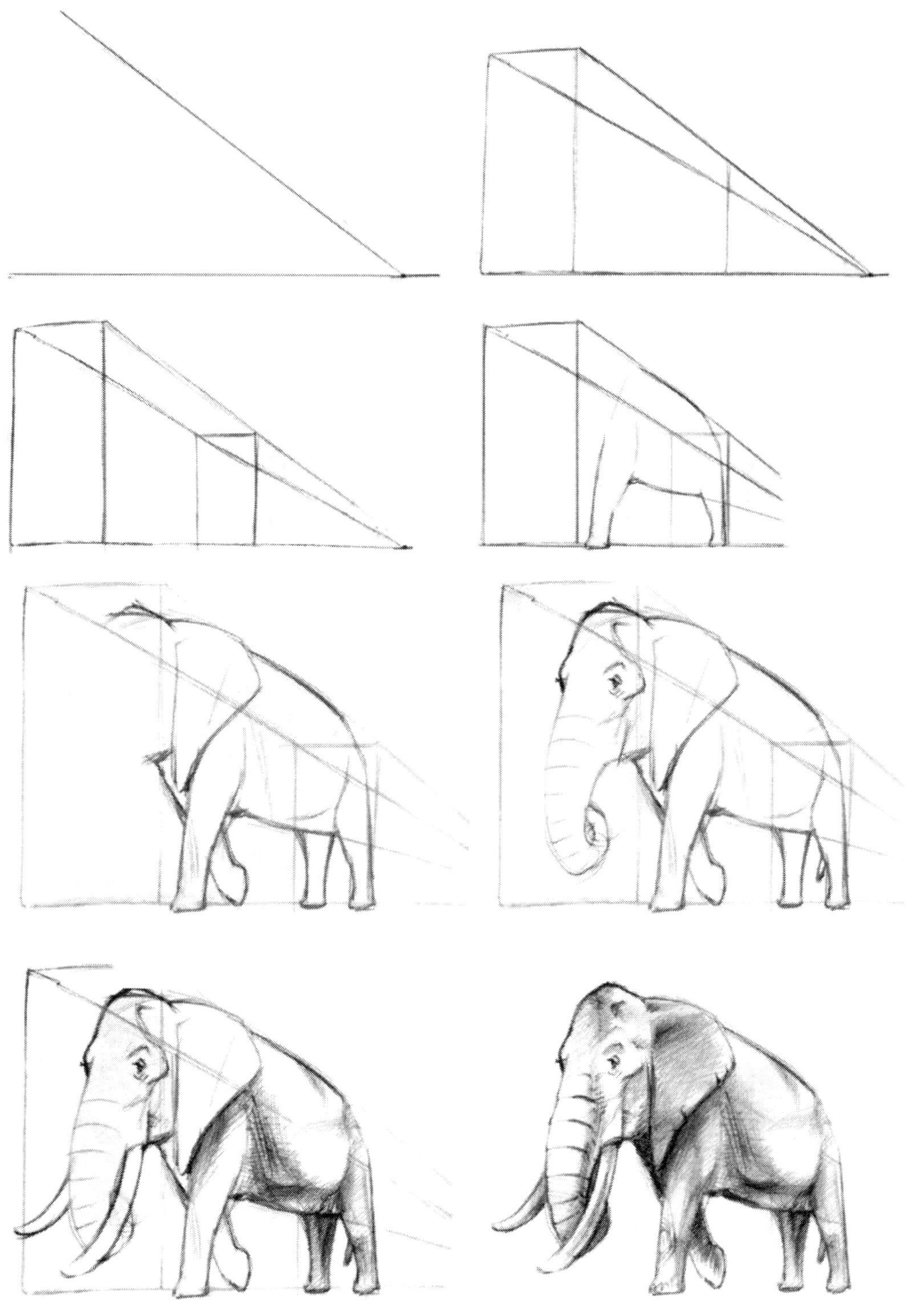

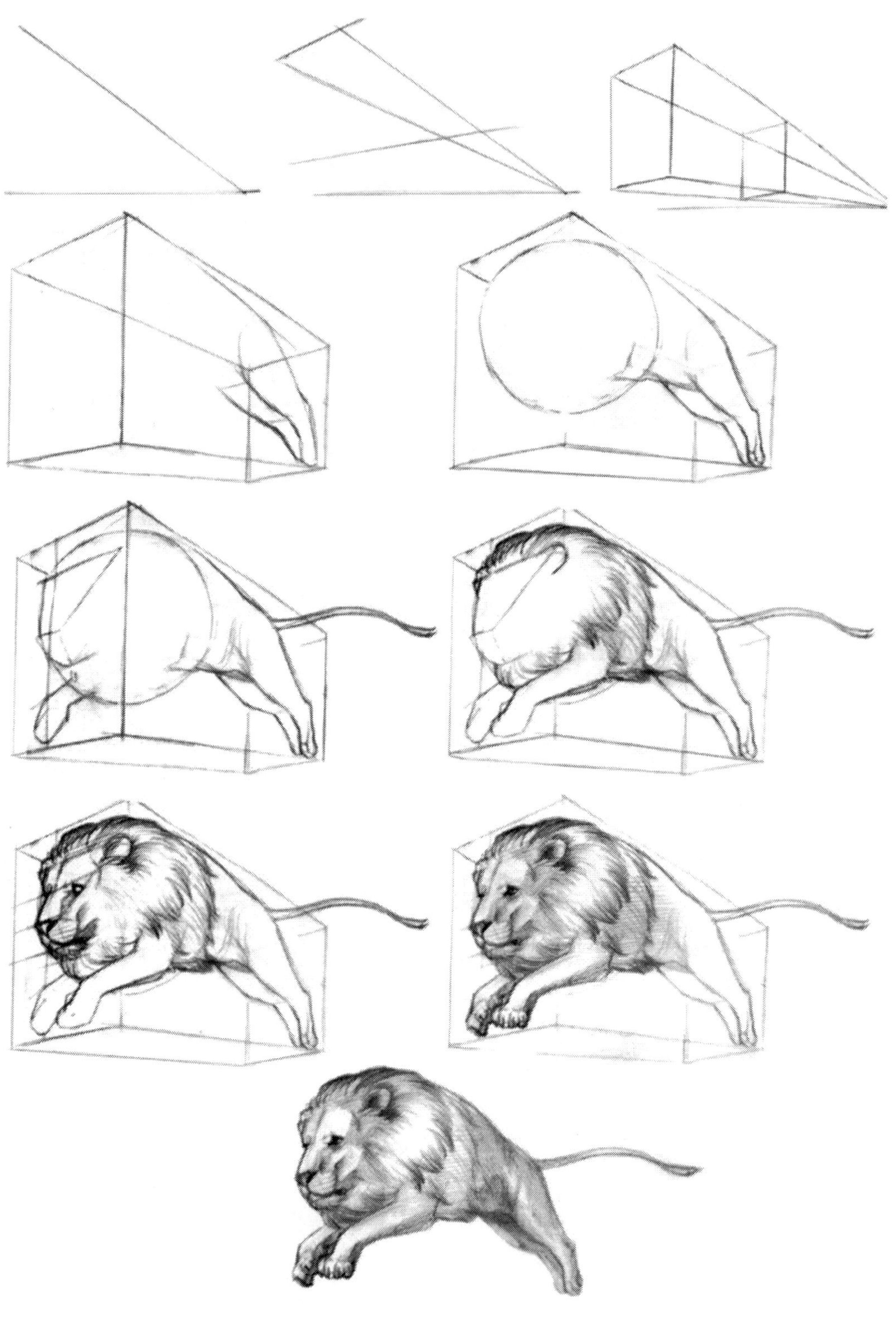

Chapter 9 – People

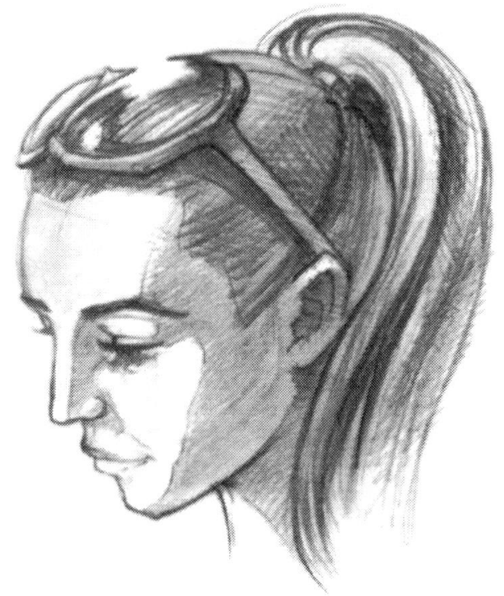

If there is one thing people point to for the reason they wanted to learn how to draw, it would want to learn how to draw the human body. People are the most difficult subjects to draw due to the slight differences in one person's body alone. The body is not symmetrical. This means, in order to make a drawing of a person realistic, you can't draw the human figure perfect in every way. It has flaws:

- One foot is wider than the other.

- One eye normally opens wider than the other.

- Your hands don't match.

There are more examples, but you get the idea.

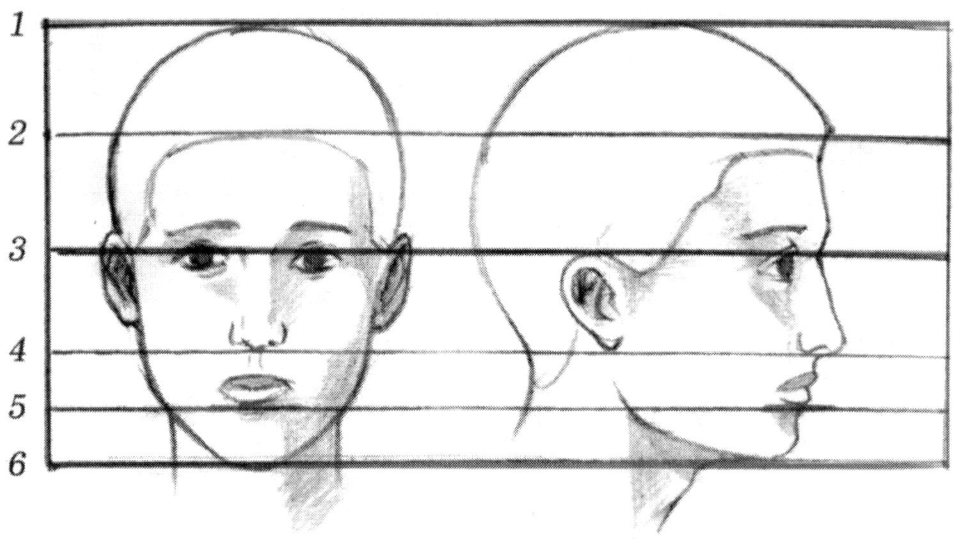

1 Top of the head

2 Hairline

3 Eyes line

4 Nose line

5 Mouth line

6 Chin

Take time to really study the diagram above. Each of the lines in the picture is guides to where the facial features are placed. Take note of three things:

1. How the hair makes the head look bigger.
2. The distance between the forehead and the eyes.

3. The distance between the bottom of the nose in relation to the lips and chin.

The female head

1. Start with a circle.

2. Draw a curved line down on the left side of the circle to start on the face.

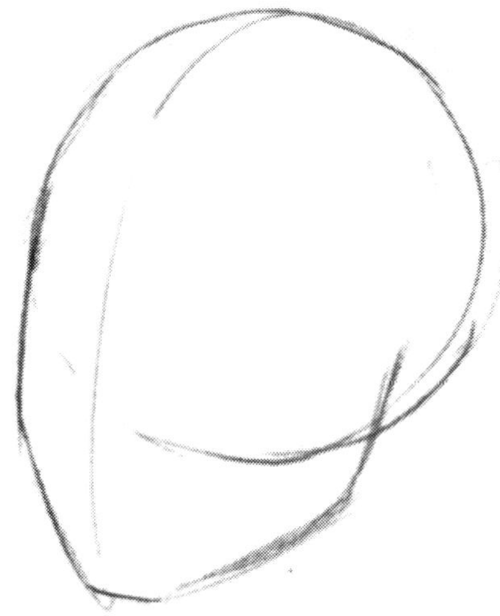

3. Curve the lines back up for the bottom jaw.

4. Using the diagram you studied, draw the lines for the features on the face first.

5. Add in the start of the nose.

6. Add the ridges for the details.

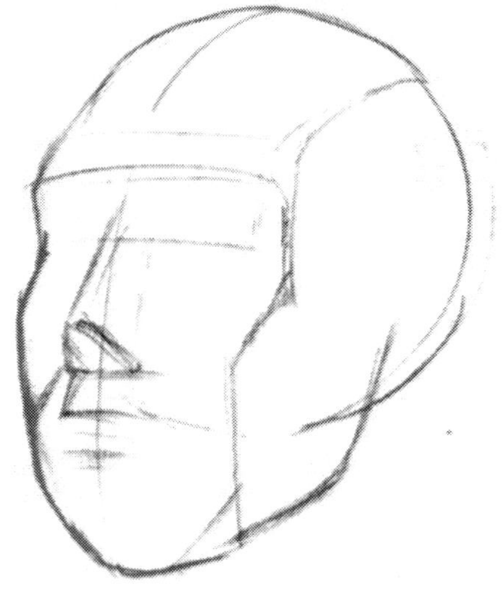

7. Draw in the brows.

8. Draw the curves for the eyes.

9. Add in the mouth.

10. Add the nose details.

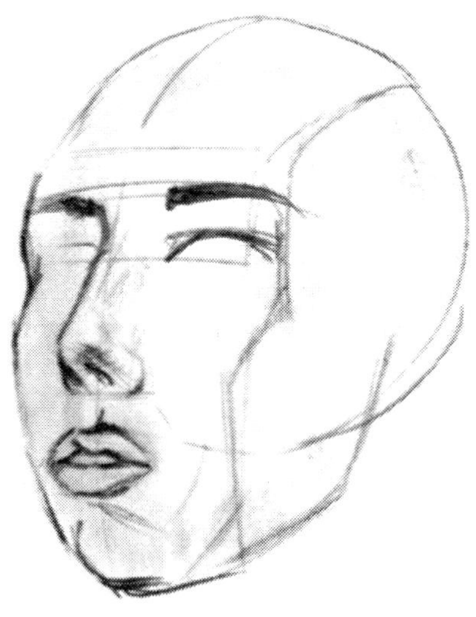

11. Add in the eye details.

12. Start adding in some of the shading.

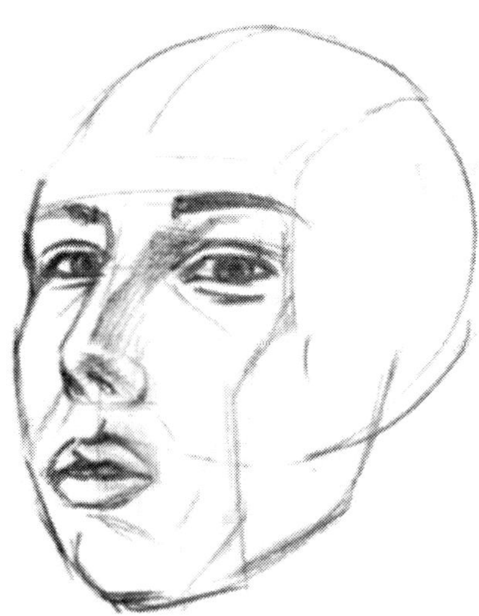

13. Add to the shading in the place you see in the picture.

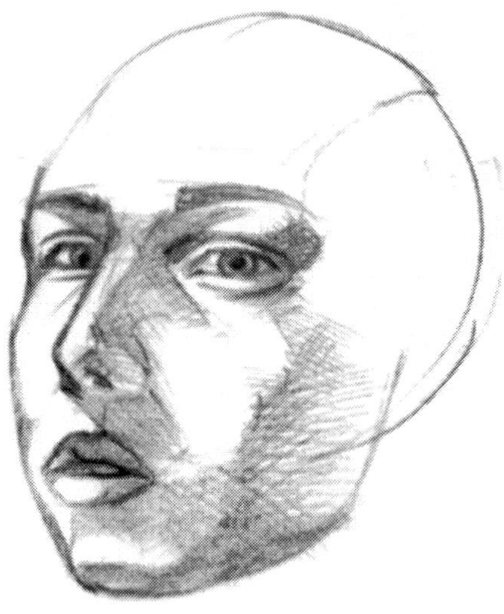

14. Draw long, sweeping curves for framing the hair.

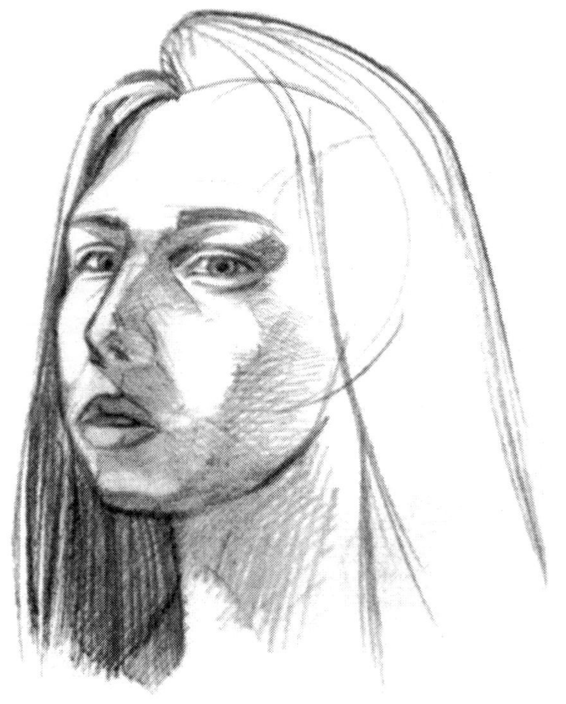

15. Shade in the hair.

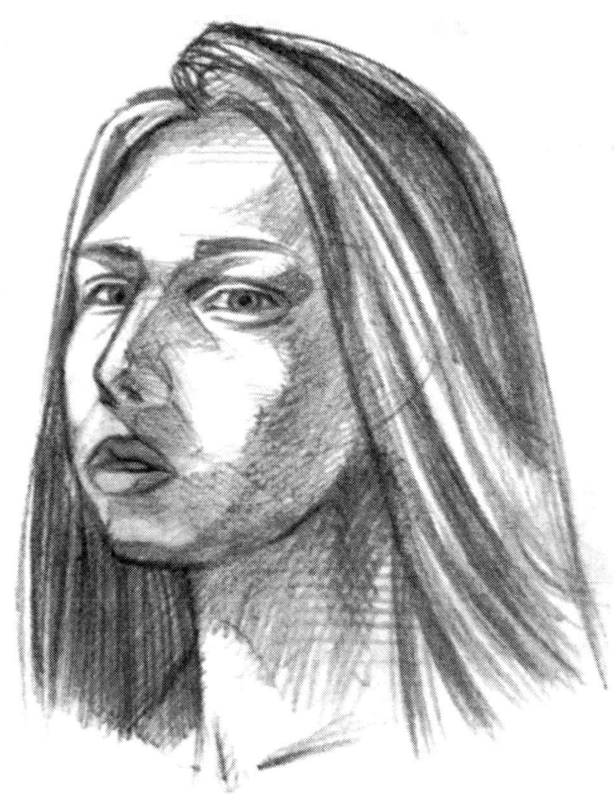

Take your time shading and smudging until you get the effect you see to the left.

Man

1. Draw the lines you see here.

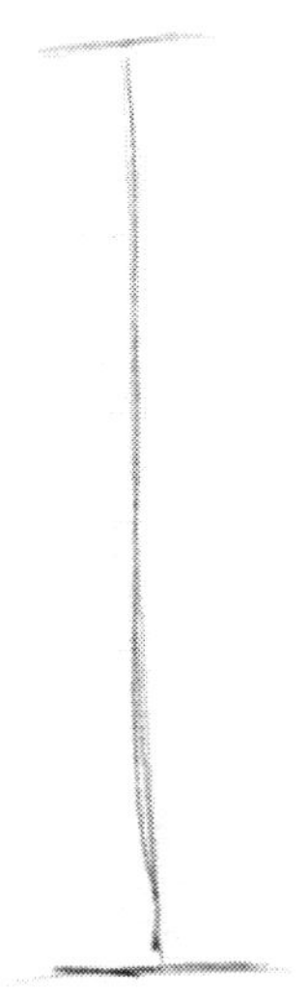

2. On the left, draw an upside-down "U" to start the head.

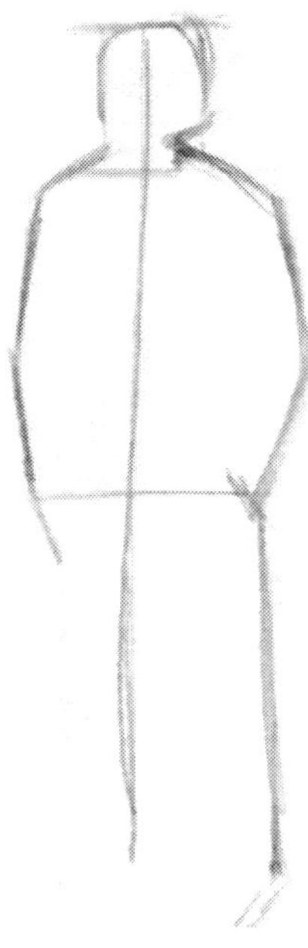

3. Lightly sketch the outline of the body.

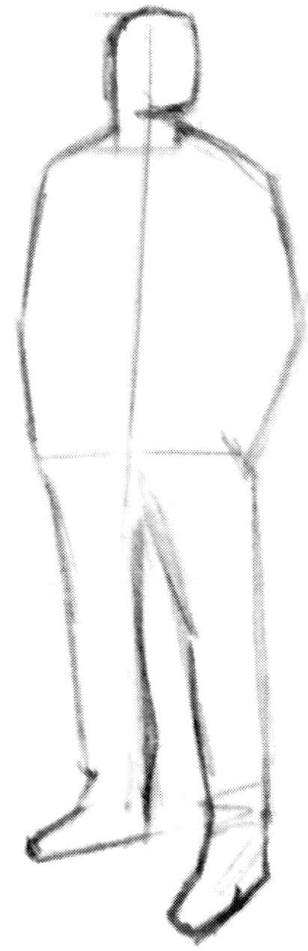

4. Close in the lines by making the heels and shoes.

5. Make the line for the hair.

6. Make the lines for the jacket. Start with the collar and make your way down.

7. Add the wrinkle lines.

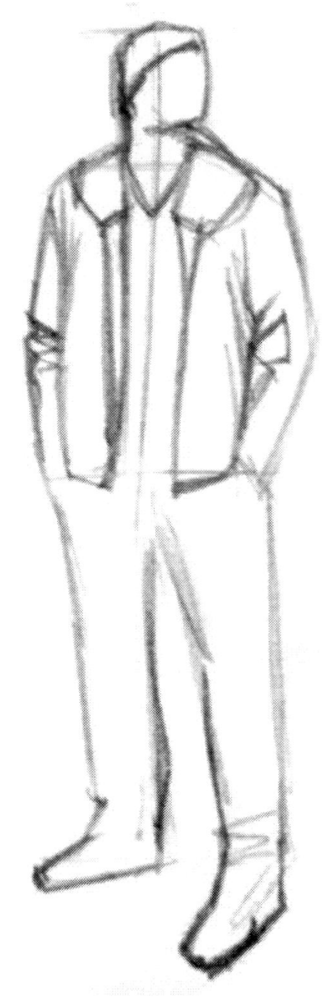

8. Add the lines for the shirt collar.

9. Add the shading in the picture on the left.

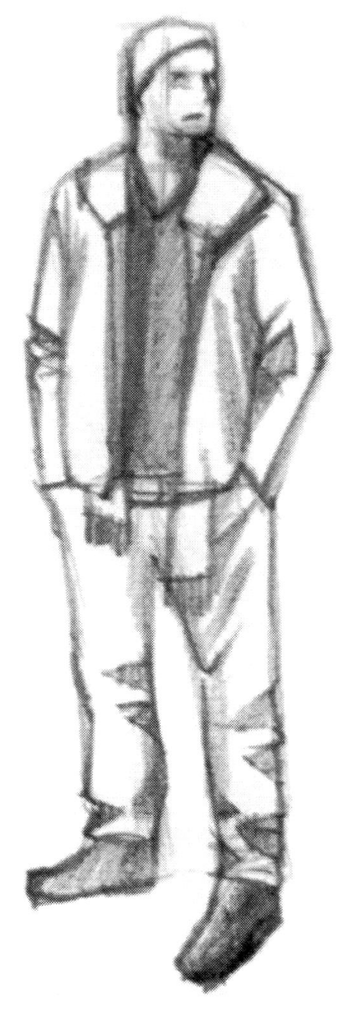

When you add in the facial features, they don't have to be as detailed as the diagram.

Woman

Follow the steps above to get started.

1. Make the curves for the pants and shoes.

2. Add the lines for the left arm.

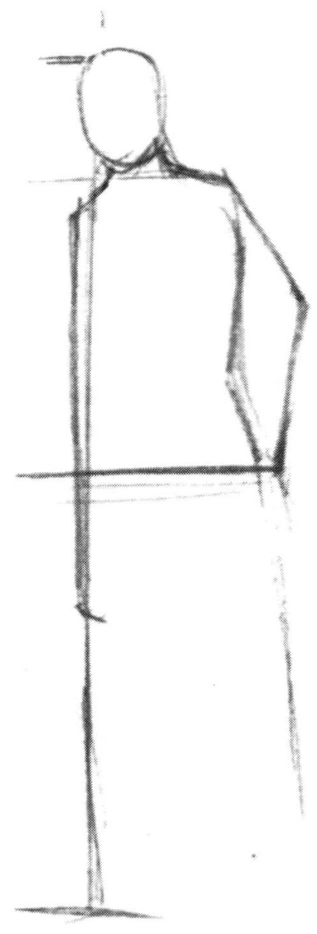

3. Add the hairline.

4. Add the details for the shoes.

5. Add the contour lines for the blouse.

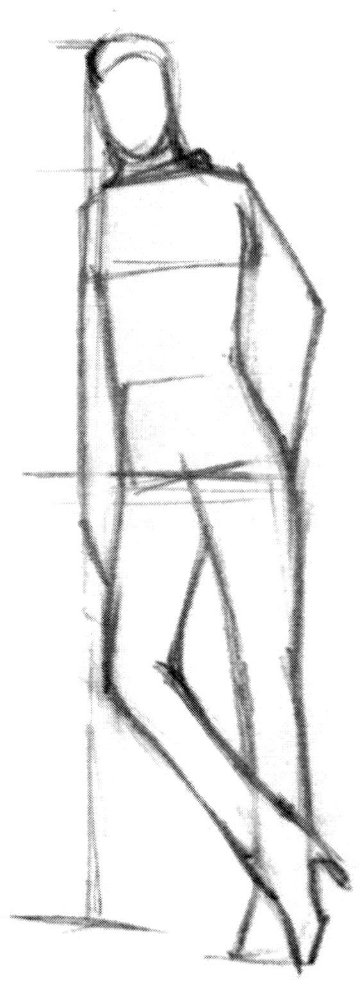

6. Add the shading you see in the picture.

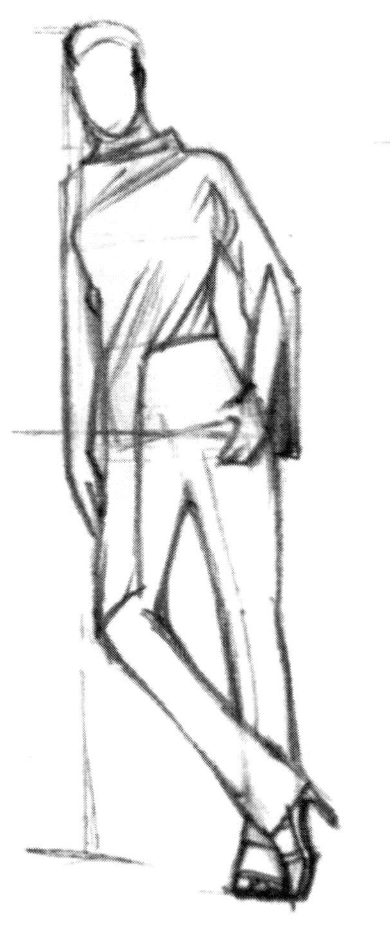

7. Add the accent lines for the pants.

8. Finish the shading.

9. Add the hair and facial features.

10. Finish the bricks for the wall.

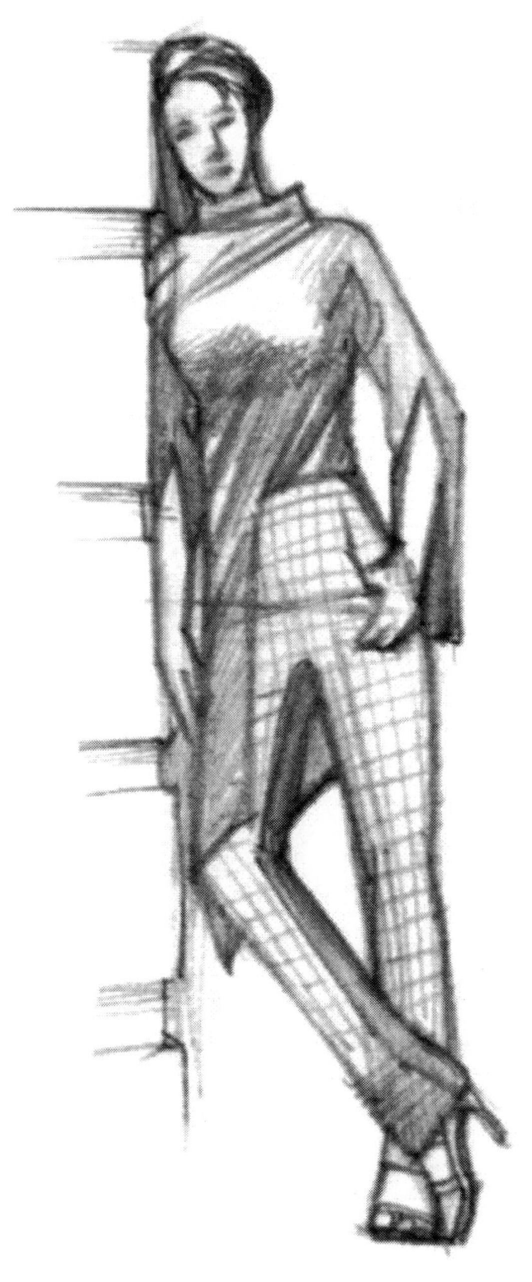

Extra practice

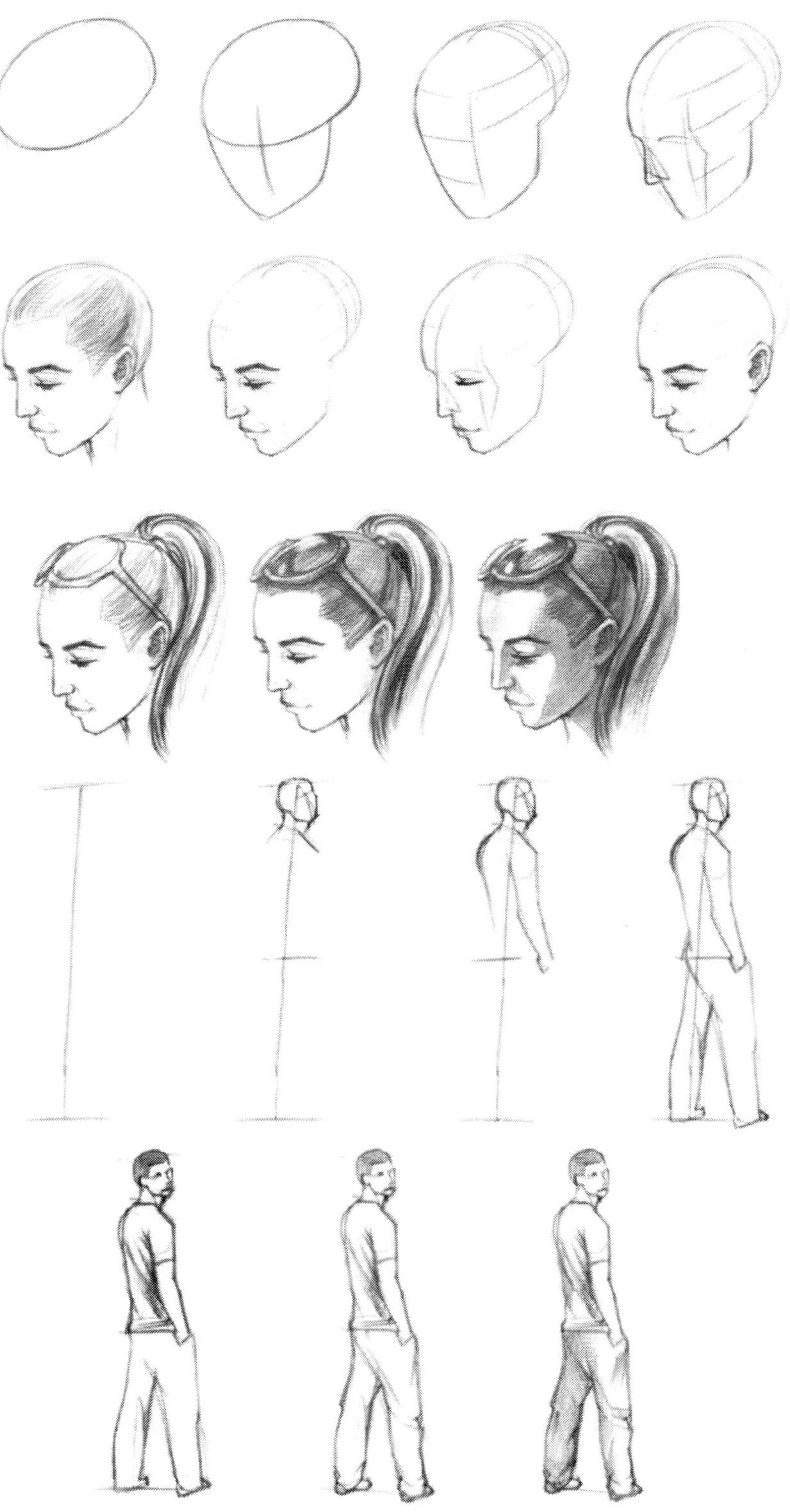

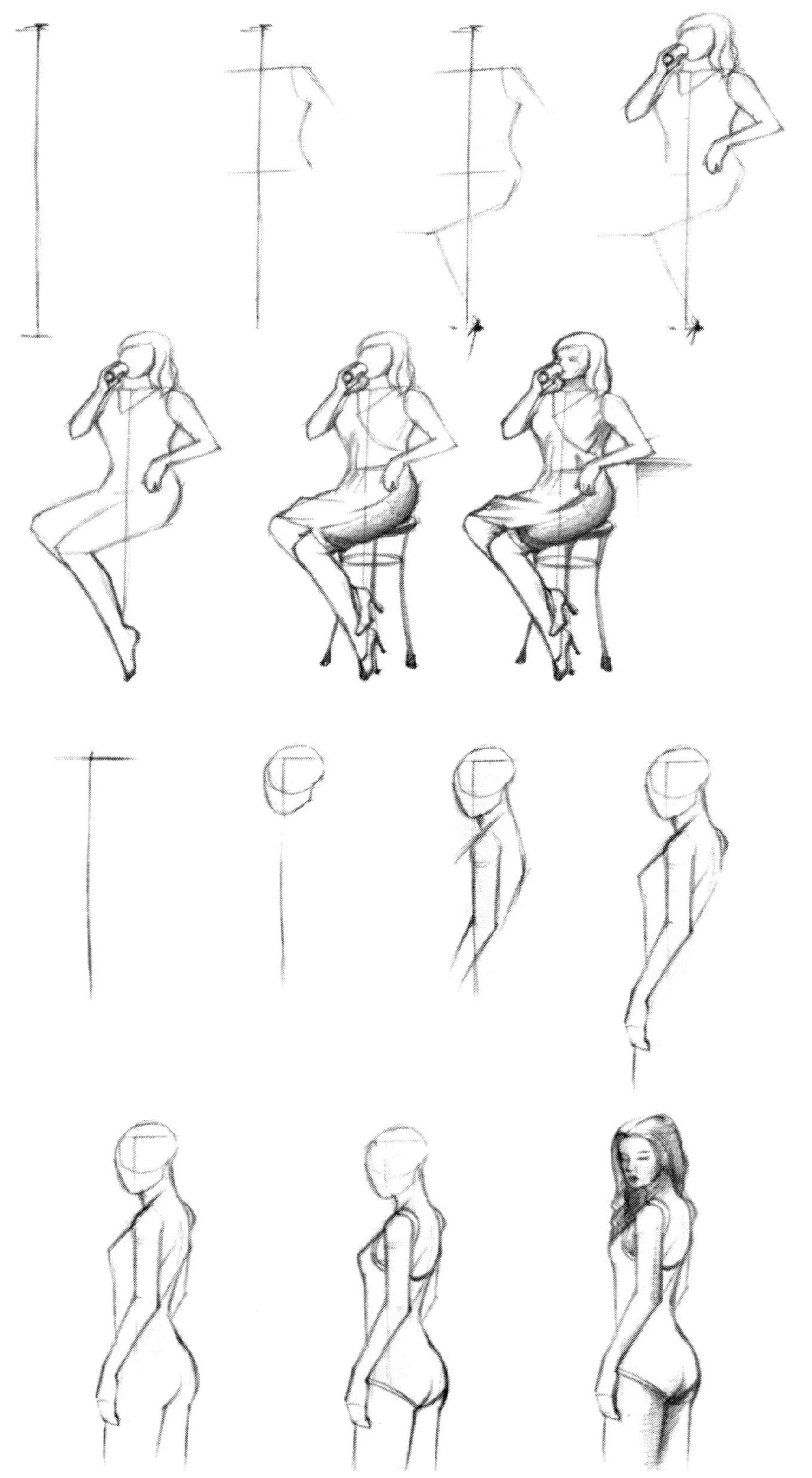

Conclusion

I hope this book has helped to get you started on your way to a new and rewarding hobby. Don't forget to challenge yourself by taking pictures and trying to draw them. Never stop improving. Until next time!

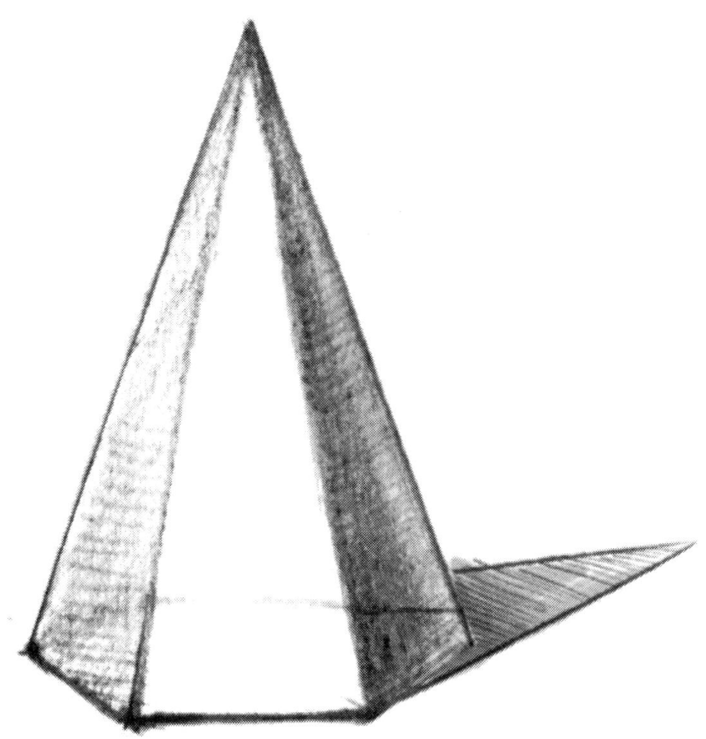

Thank you!

Thank you for choosing our book, we hope you found it interesting and helpful.

Please give us a favor to write your review.

We will greatly appreciate this!

To get a bonus – **FREE BOOK**, please send the screenshot of your review or link to this e-mail:

paul.artbooks@gmail.com and we will send to you a **FREE BOOK** in PDF as a **GIFT**!**

Hope to see you in our future books!

** **in the e-mail subject please mention the name of the book you reviewed and the author.**

If you prefer to get coloring book, please mention it in your message.

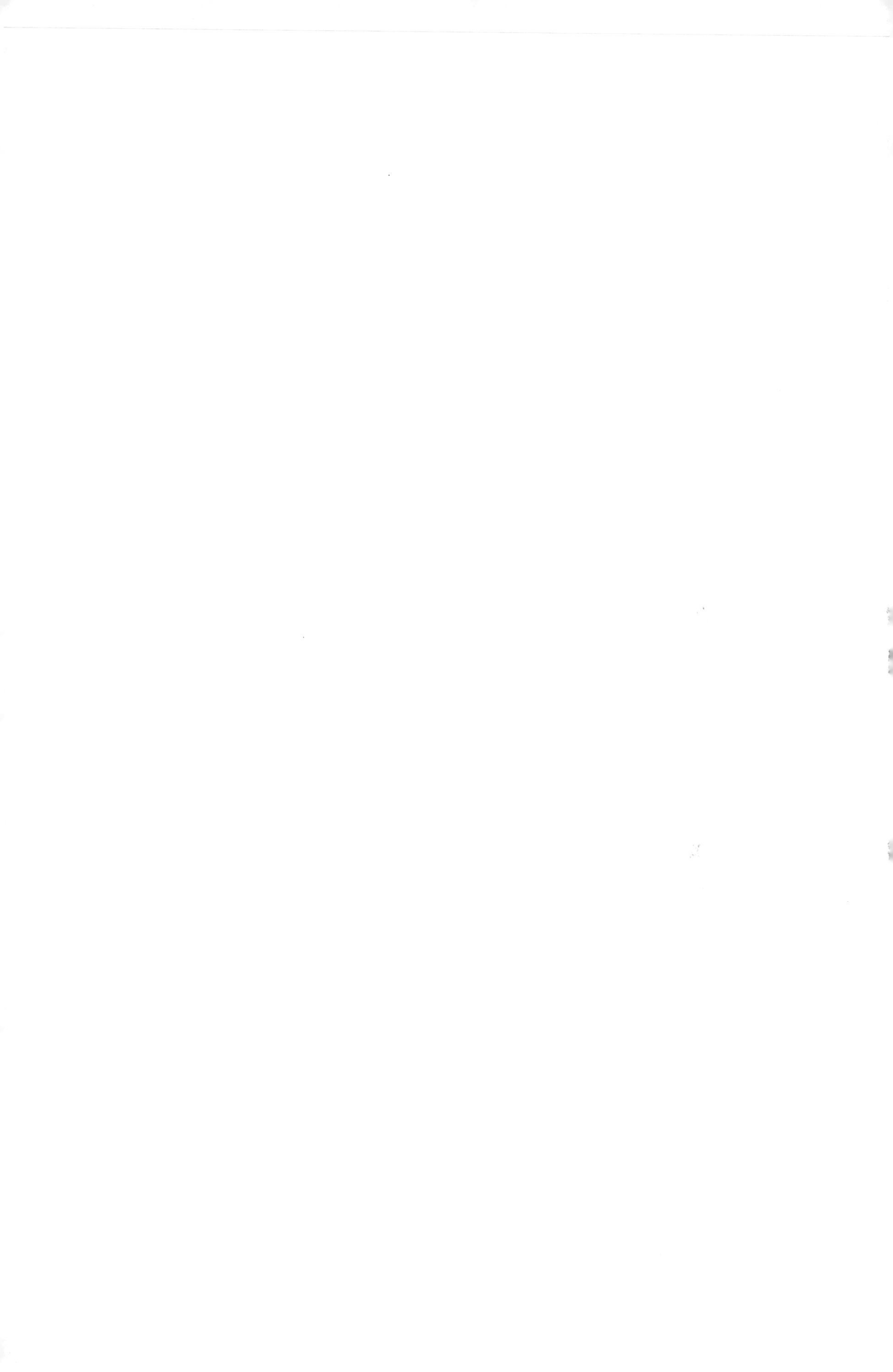

32102050R00055

Printed in Great Britain
by Amazon